SHARED WISDOM

The MIT Press's publishing mission benefits from the generosity of our donors, including Hyun-A Park and Jacob Friis.

SHARED WISDOM

CULTURAL EVOLUTION IN THE AGE OF AI

ALEX PENTLAND

THE MIT PRESS   CAMBRIDGE, MASSACHUSETTS   LONDON, ENGLAND

The MIT Press
Massachusetts Institute of Technology
77 Massachusetts Avenue
Cambridge, MA 02139
mitpress.mit.edu

© 2025 Massachusetts Institute of Technology

All rights reserved. No part of this book may be used to train artificial intelligence systems or reproduced in any form by any electronic or mechanical means (including photocopying, recording, or information storage and retrieval) without permission in writing from the publisher.

The MIT Press would like to thank the anonymous peer reviewers who provided comments on drafts of this book. The generous work of academic experts is essential for establishing the authority and quality of our publications. We acknowledge with gratitude the contributions of these otherwise uncredited readers.

This book was set in ITC Stone and Avenir by New Best-set Typesetters Ltd. Printed and bound in the United States of America.

Library of Congress Cataloging-in-Publication Data is available.

ISBN: 978-0-262-05099-9

10 9 8 7 6 5 4 3 2 1

EU Authorised Representative: Easy Access System Europe, Mustamäe tee 50, 10621 Tallinn, Estonia | Email: gpsr.requests@easproject.com

CONTENTS

PREFACE vii

I

1 **TOOLS FOR SHARED WISDOM** 3
We need to better understand human intelligence in order to design and build better social institutions.

2 **STORY-SHARING NETWORKS AND COMMUNITY INTELLIGENCE: OUR ANCIENT WISDOM** 21
Human intelligence is built on the sharing of stories. Now that AI can tell stories, what role should it have in our discussions?

3 **BRIDGING NETWORKS AND INNOVATION: THE RISE OF CULTURAL WISDOM** 39
Communities sharing stories with other communities are the engines of innovation. AI could promote discussions.

4 **CONSENSUS NETWORKS AND COLLECTIVE ACTION: MODERN WISDOM AND SCIENCE** 55
Incentives and links have created whole-of-society methods to address global challenges.

II

5 **UNINTENDED SIDE EFFECTS** 71
We are in the fourth wave of AI. I will examine how the first three changed society so we can do a better job this time.

6 **REINVENTING DEMOCRACY** 89
How can we have direct, digitally enabled democracy in the age of AI?

7 **BY THE PEOPLE, FOR THE PEOPLE** 103
Democracy for policy is good, but how do you make sure that it works on the street?

8   GETTING THERE: REGULATION AND GLOBAL COOPERATION   121
It is critical to have a consensus that supports global trade, the environment, health, and other common goods.

ACKNOWLEDGMENTS   135

APPENDIX: PREDICTION IS HARD, ESPECIALLY ABOUT THE FUTURE   137

Rational action is hard because we live in a very complex and unpredictable world. Human and animal intelligence evolved to meet these challenges.

NOTES   145

INDEX   157

PREFACE

Today we have multiple global crises unfolding and our governments seem unable to cope. Indeed, many of our social institutions feel broken. If we are to survive and thrive, we need to renovate and reimagine our societies to an extent not seen since the Enlightenment of the 1700s. If we can better understand the key ingredients that led to that Enlightenment, perhaps we can launch a new effort that will transform our societies so that we can surmount our current problems.

This book describes new science exploring the key elements that produced the Enlightenment and then uses those insights to lay out a new path. Fortunately, the green shoots and organizational tools for this path already exist; we "simply" need to put them together correctly. The key insight is that humans are not rational individuals but rather a communal, social species that builds knowledge through sharing stories, resulting in a community intelligence consisting of all the ideas, strategies, outcomes, and values that members of the community have heard about or learned through experience. Over time, parts of this community intelligence are found to be valuable by most of the community, and this forms the shared wisdom of the community. It is those stories that have broad acceptance that are the basis for successful collective action.

This process can be accelerated by technology and cultural inventions. For example, the Enlightenment seems to have emerged from the combination of letter writing for sharing theories about the world, the mechanism of citing previous work so that you can identify theories that are widely accepted, and incentives for discovering valuable new theories.

This book will begin by examining ancient examples of innovation and then ask how more recent cultural and technological innovations (e.g., broadcast media, social media, and earlier waves of AI technology) have changed human society. Understanding this history will help us figure out how we can create a flourishing, healthy human society that leverages technology like AI but also preserves individual autonomy and fulfillment, as well as how to reinvent our social institutions to encourage the development of a shared wisdom that supports our ability to make sound and informed decisions.

The second half of the book will go into more detail as to how we can use these insights to renovate our social institutions. Understanding which tools we should use and for what purposes is critical for this project. We can combine insights about the nature of human society with a deep understanding of technologies like digital media and AI in order to ask where humans and machines can best complement each other's abilities.

I have been privileged to develop long-term collaborations with thought leaders in AI, social science, and political policy, and this book draws on those unique experiences and perspectives to further the project of renovating our social institutions and making them more able to address global crises. The experimental evidence reported uses state-of-the-art data methods to study human behavior, drawn from the new discipline of computational social science. Only 20 years old, this new computational perspective has already helped launch the European privacy law discussions and shape the UN Sustainable Development Goals and the European AI regulations. This new approach to social science has led to the founding of dozens of new research labs at universities around the world and spun off health, commerce, and security companies and standards that touch billions of people daily.

I

How humans learn, build community intelligence, and develop the shared wisdom needed for collective action. Digital technology can either help or hurt.

1
TOOLS FOR SHARED WISDOM

Shared wisdom is created by sharing stories about best practices, causal connections, and critical insights among individuals, communities, and different cultures. These shared stories are like genes in our DNA because they are the building blocks of human culture. When shared stories are widely accepted within a community, they enter into the community's shared wisdom, and thus change the typical practices and beliefs of the community. This recombinant development of community wisdom is the core process that drives cultural evolution.

Over many millennia, we humans have created cultural and technical innovations such as regular campfire discussions, cities that allow diverse communities to live together, and systems for scientific literature and debate. Each of these sociotechnical innovations vastly accelerates story sharing and the rate at which shared wisdom propagates. Recent technologies, such as radio, TV, social media, and artificial intelligence (AI) have pushed the rate of sharing to levels never before imagined, and so changes in our shared wisdom happen faster than our social institutions can adapt.

A better understanding of how society creates new shared wisdom will give us the possibility of redesigning our social institutions so that they can successfully adapt to the new, extreme rates of change that we are now experiencing. At the same time, we need to better understand how new technologies and cultural innovations affect the evolution of our shared wisdom so that we can maintain the stability and human values of our society. In this book, I will share insights from current work in social science and technology, two disciplines that do not often overlap, in an effort to inspire ways to answer these pressing questions.

This book will focus on mapping out the role that we want technologies such as digital media and AI to play in our society rather than on fixing the problems of these technologies. There are already thousands of researchers and many institutions working to fix problems like bias, fairness, accountability, and all the rest. Thus, instead of suggesting patches to fix our current mistakes, this book will try to understand what world we *should* be aiming for, a world in which such problems are less frequent and can be quickly dealt with. Of course, understanding the weaknesses of both digital technologies and humans is necessary in order to build sustainable human institutions that benefit from AI and digital media. To this end, I will leverage current thinking in social science and technology as a way to frame a path forward.

STORIES OF THE PAST: COMMUNITY INTELLIGENCE

All of human history is one long search for better ways of living. Humans are not unique in this search: striving for ways to survive and thrive is the very core of evolution and is the central driver of the behavior of all species. What *is* unique about humans is our ability to tell stories. It is not just having language that makes humans special, as apes, whales, and other species not only have words but also use them in simple combinations.[1]

Stories are more than just language. They are the use of language to create shared culture and transmit experiences. They describe actions and likely consequences over time, as well as ideas about how the world works and what beliefs and behaviors we should adopt to prosper. The earliest stories were likely so simple that they were hardly worthy of the name—for example, you can find food over there, that direction is dangerous, and so on—but over the millennia they grew more complex.

Today the most widely shared human story is thought to be the hero's journey wherein a young person attempts a very difficult task that is of great value to the community, suffers serious failures, but perseveres to succeed and become a hero. This story instructs people that anyone can achieve great things, that perseverance is necessary, and that helping your community is an admirable life goal. Importantly, this sort of story appears to be critical in the successful development of children, something that more or less directly challenges conventional thinking about child development (see chapter 3).

The first human stories may have come from the marriage of song, dance, and word, leveraging our amazing mental ability to remember long sequences, such as the path for a spring migration, from just a single experience. Long stories such as the songlines of Australian Aboriginal peoples or the rhythmic epic poems of Homer define culture, communicate successful personal strategies, and explain the world in human terms. The oldest documented stories date back to the Ice Age, and there is some evidence of story transmission from ancestors who lived before that time.[2] Stories are a key part of what makes us human.

Our stories form a *community intelligence*, shaping how we look at the world and suggesting actions that will help improve our lives both today and in the future. A community consensus on the most effective actions is a community's *shared wisdom*.

WHY USE TERMS LIKE *COMMUNITY INTELLIGENCE* AND *SHARED WISDOM*?

Intelligence is defined as the ability to acquire and apply knowledge and skills.[3] The use of the word *intelligence* to describe a portfolio of stories is powerfully illustrated by today's GenAI (generative artificial intelligence). These AI models are built from a statistical summary of all the stories that people have put on the internet. The fact that this statistical repackaging of human stories can produce compelling, largely correct answers to a vast array of human questions justifies labeling this technology as AI. Similarly, the repository of stories held by human communities deserves recognition as community intelligence.

The term *wisdom* is often associated with religion, but the more modest, dictionary definition is simply the ability to use intelligence to make good decisions and judgments.[4] Shared wisdom is exactly that: the practical, behavior-oriented part of a community's culture. It is a portfolio of tools for thinking and doing, for example, the set of behaviors that people in the community use to get things done; how they search for new ideas; what they believe; what they find interesting, delightful, or abhorrent; as well as tools for prescribing the rhythms of daily life.

The process of building community intelligence and shared wisdom is continuous in that sharing stories among individuals within a community adds to the total set of ideas, strategies, and salient insights that constitute their community intelligence. When some of these stories become commonly accepted as best practice or even common sense through experience or by compatibility with previously accepted stories, they become shared wisdom. Further, when stories are generally known and accepted, it becomes easy to use them to activate collective actions that are compatible with those stories. I will elaborate on these ideas of building consensus through shared wisdom and how this leads to collective action throughout the book.

I use the term *community intelligence* instead of more familiar terms like *collective intelligence* purposely because shared concerns and circumstances are critical for productive collaborative decisions and successful collective action.[5] Communities are defined by their shared concerns and circumstances, and so they are the correct level of analysis. Community wisdom is built from a continual collective intelligence process whereby communities achieve consensus on how to address their common concerns. Connections between people are the channels along which stories, ideas, behaviors, and opportunities spread, and they are the source of most of the intelligence that permits communities and community members to act effectively.

Community intelligence is the set of ideas currently circulating, and shared wisdom is the set of ideas that have broad support within the community. Community intelligence and shared wisdom are not necessarily rational or even consistent. They are not the Truth or even the truth, but more like common sense and best practice. They are the result of a cooperative effort of *abductive reasoning*, which is the process of using stories, experiences, and data to figure out what is likely to happen in a particular situation and context, rather than deductive reasoning, which is the process of figuring out what must be logically or mathematically true.[6] This type of abductive reasoning gives communities the strategies and observations that help them survive and procreate. It is the type of intelligence that enables our species to thrive.

WHY USE TERMS LIKE *STORIES* INSTEAD OF *FACTS*?

It is also important to understand why I use the word *stories* rather than *facts*, *strategies*, or *theories*. A story is just an account of past events in someone's life or in the evolution of something.[7] Use of the word *story* emphasizes the uncertainty of our knowledge and the need to be continually skeptical of facts, strategies, and theories. The core of all current cultures was created in a prescientific world where myth and superstition ruled, and we still live in an uncertain and changeable world where yesterday's "facts" sometimes turn out to be wrong and previously reliable strategies unexpectedly fail.

The scientific terms we use today are more precise than those used by all but a few humans before 500 BCE, or by the majority of humans (and all children) even today. And, of course, we typically understand and recall facts, strategies, and warnings better when they are presented as a story.[8] When appropriate, I will refer to the more precise concepts as *stories about the past* (i.e., history), *stories for ourselves* (i.e., shared, community knowledge), or *stories for change* (i.e., plans for collective action).

Despite the modern belief that we have moved beyond myth and superstition, it is worth remembering that even today we know much less than we think we do. For example, in physics and astronomy, the oldest and arguably the most precise of the sciences, it was only recently that scientists discovered that most of the matter in the universe (i.e., dark matter, dark energy) was not part of their model of the universe.

In addition, science enters community intelligence only slowly. In the year 2000, the US National Public Radio found that 25 percent of American adults thought that the sun circles the earth.[9] We still live in a world that is filled with unknowns and uncertainties. Our culture, government, and life choices mostly turn on stories rather than logic because the social world is too complex and changeable to understand without continual observation and testing.[10]

PART I: INVENTIONS THAT HAVE ACCELERATED CULTURAL EVOLUTION, AND HOW DIGITAL TECHNOLOGIES CAN HELP OR HURT

This book is divided into two major parts. The first half sketches out how our social practices have evolved to help us develop better working knowledge, decide on best practices, and take collective action. The second part of the book will suggest how to apply these ideas to reform government and regulations. Normally our stories of the past—the typical history book, for instance—focus on big events or new sorts of tools, such as the sacking of Rome or the invention of steel. But this concrete, physical perspective misses the underlying driver of innovation.[11] I think that the more important perspective is understanding how certain cultural inventions enhanced our individual and community intelligence because it was these new patterns of thinking and understanding that generated the new tools and big events.

In this book I concentrate on three ancient cultural and technological inventions that have supercharged our biological capacity for individual and social learning. These inventions improved our ability to share stories with our entire community, to discover new stories, and to reach consensus on which stories were useful and which were not. They enabled greater rates of innovation and radically improved our community intelligence and shared wisdom, thus providing the basis for more effective collective action. The consequences of developing better story-sharing, discovery, and consensus methods were possibly the most profound changes in human history, arguably enabling the original spread of humanity out of Africa, the rise of cities and civilization, and the burst of creativity known as the Enlightenment.

Each of these notable innovations can be conceived of as networks: (1) networks for exchanging stories and building community intelligence; (2) networks for bridging between communities and building social capital; and (3) networks for achieving a consensus that enables collective action. They each transformed human life by changing our patterns of story sharing and altering incentives for consensus.

The overwhelming power of these cultural inventions to increase the pace of human innovation raises the possibility of using technologies like digital media and GenAI to augment these very human patterns of storytelling. It is hopeful that the most successful applications of GenAI that have been evaluated to date are those that help humans to better incorporate other people's work and to consider a broader range of possibilities.[12]

The first half of this book explores these three ancient cultural inventions and the social science behind them in some depth, and it considers where digital technologies may help or hurt these core human competencies. The second half of the book then builds on these ideas and suggests how technologies such as digital media and GenAI may aid in building better social institutions and governance.

STORY-SHARING NETWORKS AND COMMUNITY INTELLIGENCE: OUR ANCIENT WISDOM (CHAPTER 2)

For millions of years there was little change in how the human species lived. Then, I suspect, the social innovation of having regular story sharing within larger groups radically changed the rate of exploration and innovation.

Story-sharing networks are stereotypically exemplified by hunter-gatherer bands sharing around campfires at the end of the day. This community behavior, which does not appear to be innate, allows everyone to hear daily stories of success, danger, and opportunity from people with similar concerns and capabilities, and it consequently allows more effective combinations of individuals' stories into a group consensus.[13] Harnessing fire helped feed the body and grow the brain, but maybe more significantly, it was the stories shared around the campfire that fed the mind.

Today we have digital media for sharing stories, and while they have been very successful at spreading stories, they have been famously unsuccessful at creating the sort of shared wisdom that enables productive collective action. Much of the problem lies in the incentive mechanisms of these digital platforms, which encourage cascades of sharing around the most alarming and controversial items. In this chapter (and later in chapters 3 and 5), I discuss how this happens and how it might be fixed. Designs for improved digital media depend on enforcing more equal influence for everyone, interfaces that promote more deliberation and less immediate response, and more community input. Interestingly, commercial digital platforms are beginning to take steps in this direction with systems like community notes, which allow commentary on postings, but much work remains to be done.

BRIDGING NETWORKS AND INNOVATION: CULTURAL WISDOM (CHAPTER 3)

When stories are shared only within a single community, it creates echo chambers and hampers innovation. The second major invention in story sharing was the emergence of bridging networks that enabled stories to diffuse between different cultural groups. This was accomplished by the adoption of cultural and technological innovations such as festivals and cities that allowed different communities to more frequently intermingle and made it easier to share stories across community boundaries. This, in turn, created the ability for larger groups of people to carry out coordinated collective action.

The first civilizations, circa 11000 BCE, started to form when many different groups began to live in closer proximity, perhaps to take advantage of festivals and religious ceremonies. The trend to greater proximity continued with the development of early cities. While living closer together caused difficulties in food production, disease, and other aspects of life, festivals, cities, and the like enabled better bridging networks between communities, and this brought innovations that allowed populations to grow faster than they previously had.

Today, we still spend very substantial resources to enhance our bridging networks by attending festivals and religious gatherings and have added business conferences and retreats to our repertoire of methods for story sharing. Gatherings require expensive travel and a pause in daily activities, while cities remain expensive, dirty, and dangerous. That said, more people attend gatherings than ever before, and people still choose to live in diverse communities due to the opportunities such proximity creates.[14]

Today society is exploring digital bridging networks as a way to improve the diffusion of stories in gatherings and in cities. This chapter will explore how newer and older types of AI (e.g., machine learning, advanced statistics, or rule-based "expert" systems) are already beginning to be used to improve inclusion and build social capital in cities. AI tools that incorporate more community context and greater sensitivity to community values are what I call *stories for ourselves*, or *what do my peers do?*

Discovering new stories that may be useful has always been difficult. Augmenting bridging networks presents a great potential opportunity for technology such as social media and AI if we can use it to better share useful stories across communities. One hurdle is that stories that work for one community may not work for others. Another hurdle is privacy. Consequently, it is important that there is now privacy-preserving technology to help find people and communities that share many of your concerns because people with many shared concerns are much more likely to have experiences that are valuable to each other.[15] The ability to know community concerns and sensitivities when deciding where to build roads, place schools, and invest, without violating personal privacy, may transform governments to both be more evidence based and also hold less private citizen data.

CONSENSUS NETWORKS AND COLLECTIVE ACTION: MODERN WISDOM AND SCIENCE (CHAPTER 4)

The social inventions of regularly sharing stories with each other, and living close to other communities so that a broader range of stories was easily available, resulted in a major increase in the rate of human innovation. However, the increases in innovation resulting from these earlier social inventions pale in comparison to those caused by the most recent major advance in story sharing.

This cultural invention is the creation of *consensus networks*, which provide a documented network of story sharing across entire societies and, critically, a strong incentive for communities with common interests to reach a consensus. These new story-sharing networks have proved a reliable way for a society to rapidly develop a new type of shared wisdom that we today call science and evidence-based policy. These networks share several common features: they leverage the technologies of writing and mathematics to reduce the difficulty of conversations across time and distance; they include mechanisms for provenance and reputation that still function when people cannot physically interact; and, perhaps most critically, they provide strong incentives for finding consensus.

Modern consensus networks began around 1500 CE when scholars began to send letters to each other, trading stories (e.g., theories, observations, speculations) in order to better understand how the world works. The development of a reliable postal service and the use of letters to trade stories was quickly formalized into story-sharing organizations such as the British Royal Society and the Académie Française, which not only memorialized scientific stories but also established the tradition of referencing other people's work.

The innovation of citing other people's work provides an important incentive for contributing stories that build a consensus since contributors of such popular stories were (and still are) rewarded with career advancement and sometimes lucrative prizes or opportunities. The invention of consensus networks provides the infrastructure needed for a society-wide community intelligence, creating huge networks of stories that continually evolve as people with similar interests contribute their stories. It was, I believe, the primary enabler of the Enlightenment and still powers scientific progress today.

Today the use of modern digital technologies to provide broader context for participants seems very promising: think of something like Google search but much better tuned to capture the stories of specific scientific or technical communities. Such a community-sensitive AI search engine, which I will refer to as *stories for change* or *how can we work together?*, would also be useful to help human participants better understand the perspectives of other humans. In addition, I will examine how new computational methods can be used to analyze consensus networks in order to provide new insights into trends in science, technology commercialization, and common law.

PART II: USING DIGITAL TECHNOLOGIES TO BUILD NEW SOCIAL INSTITUTIONS THAT SUPPORT COMMUNITY INTELLIGENCE, SHARED WISDOM, AND COLLECTIVE ACTION

Our social institutions rather desperately need some sort of help. The core of many of our problems is that they are increasingly unable to keep up with the accelerating rate of technological and social change. Moreover, the rate of change is likely to continue to accelerate as people become more and more connected through digital communications, travel, and trade.

One reason our institutions are failing is because they were built using eighteenth- and nineteenth-century views about human behavior and social structure. Beginning with philosophers like René Descartes and inspired by inventions such as steam engines and spring-powered clocks, the dominant view was that human society could be understood as a huge mechanical system, ticking along like some eternal, all-encompassing clockwork. In addition, the popular view derived from theories by thinkers such as Adam Smith and Charles Darwin was that competition was the clock spring that drove both economic and political progress. Consequently, most of our social institutions were designed to keep the gears of our social institutions locked together and the springs of competition wound tight.

However, as Adam Smith explains in his often-neglected book *The Theory of Moral Sentiments,* society is not only about competition but also about community collaboration: People also cooperate and learn from each other in order to innovate, and it is this trading of favors and ideas that makes society responsive to individual needs and capabilities.[16] Our current social institutions, unfortunately, largely ignore the patterns of how people connect with other people and deploy systems and technology that treat people as if they make decisions completely independently of each other.

Given Smith's emphasis on cooperation and mutual learning, it seems to me that he might have recommended that we focus AI technology on connecting us to each other in order to help with the sharing of favors and ideas. It is worth reflecting that many of the biggest successes from older types of AI are those that help connect us to other people. When we search for driving directions, that is 1960s AI at work. When we book a flight, the algorithms that serve us use 1980s AI.

Perhaps most significantly, when we turn to the web for answers, our searches use AI from the early 2000s to connect us to what other people have said on the subject. Despite its limitations and problematic features, this sort of AI search is a human-to-human collaborative learning process that can enhance our intelligence by showing the popular consensus on facts, beliefs, strategies, and behaviors.

It is critical to remember that when members of different communities deliberate together, they can often find solutions that are better than any one individual could come up with and they can better adapt to new situations.[17] One of the major mistakes of today's social media and AI is that they implicitly consider everyone to be part of the same community. In finding solutions to problems, it is critical to focus on communities with shared interests because solutions that work for one community may not work for everyone, so we must avoid this sort of mistake and develop methods of choosing stories that foster better cross-community discovery and deliberation.[18]

Today's science tells us that it is indeed person-to-person trading of favors, stories, and collaborative effort that builds shared wisdom about what actions to take.[19] Sharing stories and cooperating produces the bridging and bonding social capital needed to recruit people for collective action. It is this accumulation of more effective community intelligence, distillation of shared wisdom, and accumulation of social capital that has allowed our species to survive during the last 20,000 years through an Ice Age, eight degrees Centigrade of climate change, 400 feet of sea rise, and increasingly frequent pandemics, wars, and ecological disasters.[20]

The recombinant storytelling process that develops new additions to shared wisdom is a far more powerful search process than simply searching the possibilities suggested by deduction from current knowledge. Just like biological evolution, it can cover a much larger space of possibilities. The ability to explore edge cases, or counterintuitive possibilities, is likely key to the continued survival of the human species.

This observation strongly suggests that we need to develop digital tools, including new types of AI, that support the human recombinant storytelling and deliberation processes rather than seek to replace human judgment. To discover a way of reaching this goal, the second half of this book begins with a brief survey of how the previous generations of AI technology (e.g., optimal resource modeling, machine learning, expert systems, etc.) have both helped and hurt society.

From this overview we can begin to draw conclusions about how we might best use new generations of AI to help reengineer our social institutions. J. C. R. Licklider, who proposed how human society and AI might work together, describes the problem as one of finding a *cooperative symbiosis* between humans and computers.[21] But today we see that the word *symbiosis* is too strong because it implies that technologies such as AI might develop into something more than just a tool for humans to use and perhaps push us in directions that are not in our best interest. So instead of the symbiotic relationship envisioned by Licklider, this book focuses on how we can develop a synergy between humans and technologies like social media or AI that preserves human autonomy and yet allows us to surmount the problems we face.

Already we have various types of digital technology everywhere: helping people search for information, giving us directions for travel, routing our messages and calls, and organizing large parts of our economy. The vast majority of adults unknowingly use simple AI technology dozens of times a day, mostly through mobile phones, and the data from these interactions are what create the current generation of AI. Like it or not, we *already* have a synergistic relationship between people, digital media, and AI tools.

Unfortunately, some of this technology has become parasitic despite being advertised as a cooperative tool to help humanity. There are serious problems with ownership of data, concentration of control, security, and bias—to name but a few problems. One of the most pernicious problems is the concentration of power in the hands of a few large companies and the most privileged parts of society.[22]

We do not have the option of just banning the use of AI because we need increasingly smarter tools to help us face complex problems like climate change and pandemics. Today, climate scientists believe that AI is critical for tracking and fighting climate change; medical scientists believe that AI is key for the discovery of new medicines; legal scholars believe it will enable much greater access to justice, and so on.[23]

The future of humanity and the development of digital technologies are bound together, and we had best make sure that it turns out as good as possible. I approach the question of how to accomplish this task by first examining the effect previous waves of technology have had on the storytelling, bridging, and consensus networks that form the core of modern societies (chapter 5), then ask how we could best shape technology to support these types of community intelligence and the formation of shared wisdom in critical tasks such as democracy (chapter 6), administration (chapter 7), and law (chapter 8). For these topics, I draw on my personal history of discussions with national leaders, experience in standards creation, and legal scholarship.

UNINTENDED SIDE EFFECTS (CHAPTER 5)

To build qualitatively better social institutions we will need to harness the power of digital media and AI, but only in ways that preserve the core human processes that create community intelligence and shared wisdom. To better understand how AI and related technologies might affect society in the future, it is useful to ask how earlier waves of AI have altered society. Consequently, this chapter of the book describes the AI boom-and-bust cycles that have occurred over the last 70 years and tries to find commonalities that may help society leverage the capabilities of AI while avoiding problems from the current and future AI booms.

REINVENTING DEMOCRACY (CHAPTER 6)
This chapter focuses on democracy, which I define as building and harnessing the collective wisdom of the entire society with the goal of creating productive, collective action. We will need to harness both digital media and AI in order to create new democratic policy mechanisms that are both more agile and inclusive. A particularly important aspect of reinventing democratic institutions is to avoid what Plato called the "Noble Lie," that is, the idea that an elite class of people should manage society in order to maintain social harmony.

BY THE PEOPLE, FOR THE PEOPLE (CHAPTER 7)
Creating more inclusive and engaging consensus platforms for policy decisions only helps decide which way to go, not how to get there. In modern societies we use a nineteenth-century model of bureaucracies to implement those policies, and the rigidity and self-interest of these bureaucracies creates enormous problems for our societies. How can we use today's better understanding of people and society, together with ubiquitous digital networks and AI, to redesign our methods for decision-making and governance so that they are more respectful of individuals and communities and yet at the same time more agile and effective?

GETTING THERE: REGULATION AND GLOBAL COOPERATION (CHAPTER 8)
What can we possibly do that will work worldwide? Our real problem in dealing with issues such as climate change or health crises is our inability to achieve and maintain the shared wisdom needed to act decisively.

Digital media and AI systems that are cooperatively synergistic may help us build the human-driven deliberation and collective action platforms we need to solve our pressing global challenges, but deploying them across different nations and different cultures is difficult.

We need to take a consensus approach, one that appeals to the short-term self-interest of all stakeholders. One way to accomplish this and address our other challenges is to leverage the shared wisdom that produced our globally interoperable health and financial networks as well as the internet itself. Key to this process is enforcing transparency and accountability through mechanisms such as openly available audit trails and clear liability regulation and enforcement.

STORIES OF THE FUTURE: WHAT SHOULD DIGITALLY ENABLED SOCIAL INSTITUTIONS LOOK LIKE?

The aim of this book is to examine the process of humans inventing new social institutions in order to improve their lives, using the perspective of cultural accumulation rather than focusing on the artifacts developed as the outputs of this social process. This book takes this human-centric point of view in order to understand what groups of people were striving to accomplish and what results were achieved rather than focusing on artifacts such as roads, bronze tools, ships, or digital technologies that were developed to support these new social processes.

The inventions of story sharing and consensus networks enhance community intelligence and shared wisdom because they make story sharing more inclusive and make reaching consensus more likely. They are aids for collective thinking that leverage tools for memory, physical devices for transmitting information, and models for scientific discovery. Humans have tried many different types of story-sharing and decision-making inventions over the millennia, including religious cults, warlords, kings, and emperors, but most of these have worked erratically if at all.

The reason we have been able to develop and try many different types of social organization is because human community intelligence is extremely flexible and enables communities to adopt a wide range of behaviors and social institutions. We should be able to adapt to AI as well in order to safely leverage the advantages AI offers us, but first we need to understand how to accomplish that goal while avoiding the dangers.[24]

The inventions of story-sharing, bridging, and consensus networks have stood the test of time and outperformed all the others. It is interesting that these three types of network innovation are ordered in size from small to large scale, and in time from oldest to youngest. This suggests an arc of progress toward ever larger and more innovative social organization. Our era's invention of digital networks and AI may be the very beginning of a fourth and potentially even more effective type of story-sharing network. The result should not be the Singularity envisioned by some technologists but a Plurality of cultures and communities.

A strong motivation for using terms such as community intelligence, story sharing, consensus networks, and shared wisdom is to emphasize that this perspective is fundamentally different than what people refer to as the standard scientific approach. The view taken here is that we understand surprisingly little of our world, and so we must use an abductive approach for our decisions rather than trying to rely on the deductive approach typical of physics or better understood domains. Further, because of the world's complexity, the key mediating structure for day-to-day decision-making is the community, and not the individual, because communities can pool experiences in order to make better decisions about their shared concerns.

This community intelligence perspective has a concrete logical and mathematical realization as an abductive reasoning mechanism built on sharing information among cooperative actors. As we will see in chapter 2, this is quite different from deductive logic or the reductionist sort of scientific analysis too often used in both the popular press and discussions about policy.

The mathematical foundation for our model of the abductive development of community intelligence has well-understood optimality properties that are particularly relevant to groups of actors with shared concerns and values and who are working together in highly uncertain environments. It is a cooperative group search among multiple and changing communities of interest.[25] Importantly, it generalizes well to the sort of ever-changing, chaotic environments that humans live in, as described in the appendix.

By connecting these mathematical and logical underpinnings to our ancient cultural inventions, we can gain a better understanding of how the development of new ways for humans to share and combine stories has transformed society in the past. The idea of human progress as the history of cultural inventions that improve story sharing offers a new perspective to analyze the problems and benefits of digital networks and AI. Further, by using this model of human decision-making to analyze the AI technologies developed during the 1960s, 1980s, and 2000s and link them to cultural changes, we can begin to see how we should adapt the current AI technologies to best suit human society.

The goal, of course, is to investigate how new technology can be combined with cultural innovation to create social systems that improve our community intelligence and shared wisdom while preserving human agency and autonomy. We also need to make it easy to shield ourselves from overly powerful actors and those with malevolent intent as well as to quickly correct unfair, biased, or unaccountable actors and processes.

What we will find is that, quite generally, new social systems and technology applications have ignored the importance of community structure in human decision-making and collective actions, and that too often human leaders have used these new systems to diminish human agency. By leveraging the ideas of community and the core human consensus processes that build community intelligence and shared wisdom, we can design digital networks and AI that have the potential to avoid the problems we experience today and provide our societies with a much greater capability for achieving rational deliberation and consensus for collective action.

2

STORY-SHARING NETWORKS AND COMMUNITY INTELLIGENCE: OUR ANCIENT WISDOM

This chapter, along with the two chapters that follow, examines how humans innovate and decide to act and how human culture evolves over time. These core mental processes have proven their worth because they have allowed us to survive through an Ice Age, catastrophic sea rise, numerous pandemics, and more. New technologies and social institutions should not short-circuit or replace these robust, essential human capabilities.

We want social institutions and technology that leave untouched our core capabilities for learning, decision-making, and cultural evolution. GenAI is of particular concern because it is a storytelling technology, and sharing stories is the basis by which people decide what the most useful actions to take are, and through which we transmit culture.

In the first half of this chapter, I discuss how humans learn from stories, how learning can turn into collective action, and how this learning-acting process affects cultural evolution. This topic is one of the most researched areas of social science, with the work of leading scientists such as Mark Granovetter, Stanley Milgram, Ronald S. Burt, Albert-László Barabási, James Evans, Joseph Henrich, and Tom Malone, to name a few of the most well known, mapping out the area.

With the advent of advanced computing and large, quantitative behavioral datasets, it is now possible to define and validate much more quantitative mathematical models of the social processes that produce innovation and collective action. The first part of this chapter describes how familiar social science work connects with these recent mathematical formulations of the human learning process. The second half of this chapter then uses the structure of these mathematical models as a guide for building tools and institutions that cooperate synergistically with humanity and avoiding those that are parasitic. This will allow the development of a taxonomy of digital tools that can help individuals decide what actions to take without removing human agency and judgment or preventing the development of social capital and trust.

STORIES OF THE PAST

It is important to remember that story sharing is at least as much for communities as it is for individuals. Perhaps the historical examples with the oldest roots are the Dreamtime songs and stories shared among the Aboriginal peoples of Australia. Their songs, known as songlines, are particularly interesting because the rhythmic nature of the songs helps make the stories more memorable. The songs and stories typically share the knowledge of local migration pathways and affordances, connecting places to creation events and ceremonies, and form the basis for ceremonies in those places.[1]

Today each Aboriginal community has a different collection of songs and stories that tell about how best to live on their land and about the history of the community. Some stories refer to large-scale events such as volcano eruptions or asteroid strikes, and so can be dated. The oldest story with a verified date is 7,000 years old, but there are also stories that seem to date to the end of the last Ice Age.[2]

The effect of these stories and songs is to create different cultures and patterns of behavior in different communities. From an evolutionary perspective, having different patterns of behavior means that it is more likely that at least one community will survive a pandemic, a change in climate, or an invasion of a competing species. Through the mechanism of storytelling, our patterns of how we interact with each other—our culture—can evolve almost as fast as changes in the environment and much faster than changes in our biology. This rapid cultural evolution has been essential to our species' survival, allowing us to endure and thrive through millennia of existential challenges.

THE ROLE OF STORIES

Why did humans evolve to make decisions using the behaviors and strategies they hear about in the stories of other people in their community?

The answer may be that this way of learning can be thought of as the cultural version of Darwinian evolution: the most useful stories survive and spread to become the basis for behaviors that are shared within a community. This creates a shared portfolio of the community's intelligence, for example, the behavioral strategies, beliefs, and values that make it more likely for the community to thrive.

Humans are prodigious storytellers, perhaps due to the importance of sharing stories for our survival. Sometime in the last few hundred thousand years humans got very good at trading stories. We remember stories better than facts, we can generalize from stories by use of analogies, and I think that there is a good case to be made that our cognitive abilities do not come from our innate capability for logic and reasoning but rather from learning stories about how to use logic and reasoning.[3]

Story-sharing networks are stereotypically exemplified by hunter-gatherer bands sharing stories around campfires at the end of the day. This collective behavior allows everyone to hear daily stories of success, danger, and opportunity from people with similar concerns and capabilities, and consequently allows for a more effective combination of individuals' stories into a group consensus. Group learning by trading stories is probably older than modern humans; for instance, great apes debate group behavior using verbal signaling.[4]

A well-known form of community intelligence in animals is found in bees. The collective organism that is the beehive—analogous to a human community—allocates some of its resources to risky, uncertain exploration in anticipation of bountiful future returns. When a worker bee finds a good patch of flowers it will return and communicate its find with other bees using a "waggle dance" that indicates the direction and distance of the flowers. This results in a consensus process whereby more and more bees visit the new flower patch, and for particularly rich flower patches this trend can grow into collective action, with the entire hive moving to the new location.[5]

In human communities, stories spread among people across their social networks, and exactly who talks to whom, along with the storyteller-listener relationship, strongly biases what stories an individual hears. The *story-sharing network*, therefore, strongly shapes a community's intelligence.[6] The effectiveness of a community's intelligence depends on whether the story-sharing network includes everyone and whether they all have compatible goals and values.[7] The importance of this type of learning is evident in today's world, with business schools and companies everywhere trying to design better story-sharing networks in order to select and spread the most effective stories.[8]

NO REGRETS: MAKING THE BEST DECISIONS

The qualitative logic of bees signaling information to each other and humans sharing stories is compelling, but there is a deeper truth that suggests that these patterns of behavior are optimal. The key realization is that this behavior is a collective search process, where groups of agents continually search for new opportunities and new, more effective behaviors.

Our proclivity for sharing stories has a survival value that helps us cope with the necessity of continually finding sufficient food and other resources and simultaneously developing better skills and strategies. Sharing stories regularly around an evening campfire, or in an office cafeteria, allows more productive collective action than less organized story-sharing patterns. Over time, regular story sharing produces a shared community intelligence about how best to find resources, avoid harm, innovate, and make achieving consensus and enabling collective action easier and faster. Unlike daily discussions about what to do next, the stories in the shared community intelligence are frequently retold, perhaps in group chants or songs, reinforcing collective norms and providing an identity story.

In unknown or uncertain environments there is always the question of how much effort to spend on familiar daily activities and how much effort to spend on finding new, better ways of living. People base most of their decisions on their community's shared wisdom, which is the compilation of the beliefs, strategies, norms, and goals that most members of the community have adopted. Nobel Prize winner Daniel Kahneman refers to reliance on your community's intelligence as *system 1 thinking*, allowing a fast, often reflexive choice of behaviors from your portfolio of common behaviors.[9] This portfolio evolves over time through individual experience and story sharing with other community members, and it decisively shapes the vast majority of our actions. It is therefore critical for survival of individuals in the community.

Is the compilation of stories enough to account for human intelligence? Today's large language models, such as ChatGPT, are trained on volumes of human-written stories and produce answers by following the statistics of those stories. The fact that these AI systems are nearly as good as humans on many tasks shows that the combination of many stories is at least a first approximation of the sort of human fast thinking Kahneman calls system 1 thinking. It is probably not good enough to account for reflective deliberation, which Kahneman calls *system 2 thinking*, but many researchers suspect that placing system 1 thinking in a reflective feedback loop will provide human-level thinking generally.[10]

There are also some powerful mathematical results concerning the practice of combining personal and community evidence. Done correctly, it allows both the individual and the community to achieve optimal, minimum-regret decision-making. The criterion of minimum regret means that an agent or group of agents makes the best decision possible at each instant given the information and previous experience available at the time. It is doing the best you can do.

Classic minimum-regret decision-making is often referred to as a *bandit problem* because of the formal equivalence to the question of which slot machine (i.e., "one-armed bandits") to try in a gambling casino. In the last decade, the mathematical solution to such problems has been extended to distributed agents; for example, a gambler observes the payouts of other casino patrons and combines those observations with personal knowledge to decide which slot machine to try next. This is a clear analog to individuals in a hunter-gatherer group observing others to learn what does and does not work in that environment.

The importance of these mathematical results is that they provide a strategy that a group of agents may use to form an optimal, minimum-regret policy for action. The core of this strategy is for each agent to use a store of community intelligence to estimate the prior probability of success for a potential action. Next, each agent uses this prior probability to moderate the probability of success as learned from personal experience, which then determines the posterior probability of success for the potential action. The agents then typically choose the action most likely to work, but because of the need to minimize uncertainty and maximize reward, they must also learn more about their environment. This means that they must experiment with actions that have uncertain rewards and even try actions that are unfamiliar. This trade-off is known as the *exploit-explore dilemma*—known strategies should be used for surviving, but the search for better strategies is needed for continued thriving.

To see how this works concretely, consider the bee example. At the start, a hive member makes the decision to leave the hive and search for a new flower bed (i.e., tries an unfamiliar and uncertain action). Most other bees observe the excitement of that bee when it returns (so they can estimate the likelihood of this being a significant discovery) but have also learned through experience that great new flower beds are rare (i.e., the prior probability is low) and decide not to try out the new flower bed (i.e., their posterior probability used to select actions is to do nothing). However, some bees do try the new flower bed (perhaps young ones with less experience and more optimistic prior probabilities), and as more and more returning bees are seen to be excited, the likelihood eventually overwhelms the prior, and all the bees begin to visit the new flower bed.

This strategy for optimal, minimum-regret decision-making has demonstrated excellent performance in many domains, enough so that it is a standard approach in domains such as signal processing, medical decision-making, and finance. It shows good generalization to new and changing situations and the ability to work with noisy, long-tailed, and ill-conditioned data inputs.[11] If the agent is smart enough to be capable of a little mental reflection, it can also handle situations where some agents have different, even adversarial, goals. Agents decide who they should trust to be part of their learning (story-sharing) network by comparing the choices they have made to the choices of the other agents and, from that comparison, selecting the best subset of agents with whom to trade stories.[12]

HUMAN RATIONALITY

We know people tell stories, and the decision framework described in the previous section provides an explanation about why this behavior evolved—but do people really do this? Could this be how human communities have been able to survive previous challenges such as sea rise, wars, crop failures, and pandemics?

A good place to begin answering this question is by examining large-scale experiments about how people make financial decisions. The advantage of examining personal investment decisions is that here we can easily analyze how people made their decisions, measure whether each decision was good or bad, and look at the long-term results after people have made hundreds of investment decisions. The long-run results are critical because sometimes it only takes one really bad decision to wipe out a person's investment portfolio. By understanding how people make decisions with their personal money, we can better understand how groups of people can make better, more reliable decisions in other areas.

INDIVIDUALS AND ROLE MODELS

To answer these questions about how individuals and groups can make consistently good decisions, my colleagues and I conducted a large, global experiment that examined the decisions in a community consisting of hundreds of thousands of regular people investing their own money using an online investment platform called eToro.[13] The eToro platform is unusual because users can see how other people are investing, see how it worked out for those investors, and then learn from their examples. Like early humans trading stories around a campfire, users of eToro can readily learn from others' stories. For instance, eToro has a leader list consisting of people whose investment strategies have done the best over the last few days, and the eToro investors can use these people as role models to guide their personal investments. In fact, this is often a great thing to do because the leader list is almost always composed of role models that will do well over the next short period of time.

Because eToro is set up to make investment strategies and outcomes transparent, social learning is easy. The behavior of people using this platform is much more like the story sharing that happens in everyday life than it is the everybody-invests-in-secret model of most investment platforms. Learning from the experiences of friends and coworkers is natural to humans, and eToro provides a similar sort of story-sharing experience.

What we discovered when we watched the behavior of hundreds of thousands of people from all around the world (remember that everything is visible in eToro) was that people who make investment decisions all by themselves generally do not do well. In the language of economists, they are not *rational*. Informally, rationality means knowing what you want and how to get it. Isolated people know what they want (more money) but are bad at figuring out how to get it.

On the other hand, people who actively investigated other people's investment strategies and incorporated their role models' judgments about what strategies were good into their own strategy did much better. Importantly, we found that groups of people that actively learned from each other are *collectively rational*; that is, a community of people with similar goals who are sharing strategies typically develop a shared wisdom made up of a set of reliably good strategies. Even though their aggregate financial strategies are reliably quite good, individually they sometimes adopt poor strategies. In other words, the users of eToro form a very successful community intelligence that makes reliable decisions, but individuals are sometimes too stubborn or opinionated for their own good.

STORY SHARING IMPROVES INVESTMENT

This result is exactly what we would expect on the basis of our minimum-regret decision model. It may seem surprising that a story-sharing network of individually limited naive people can together develop wise investments. One reason for this is that even if an individual is smart and diligent, they can only test and evaluate a small number of investment possibilities. Having examples from the rest of the community is a great way to learn about many more possibilities.

Sometimes, people fail to learn from others due to self-segregation. Users who are new to eToro, for instance, often begin by learning only from people who have the same nationality or same gender. This tendency to follow only your tribe turns out to be a poor strategy because it does not capture a sufficient diversity of experience. The fact that the traders that explore consistently perform well shows that an AI analysis of the eToro strategy-sharing network would allow the selection of a set of investments that are quite reliable. The lesson here is that reliable decision-making requires knowing the outcomes of many different stories, and communities with a good story-sharing network can use the collective outcome data to make wise decisions.

This result implies that if individual investors could hear more different stories they would do better. With machine learning, GenAI makes this relatively easy to do. One simply prompts the AI with the investments an investor has recently considered and then it searches for what other uncorrelated investment strategies have not been considered. On eToro we found that the typical investor uses only around three different strategies. By prompting the investor with additional strategies, their return on investment rises dramatically. Interestingly, this performance increase peaks at about ten strategies total; beyond that, the investor is likely to be overwhelmed with information.[14]

WHAT ABOUT EXPERTS?

The eToro experiments illustrate that average people depend on the people around them to make good financial decisions, but what if experts who are trained in the mathematics of finance and have decades of experience are different? Could they be true "rational individuals" and not the social explorers that populate eToro? To answer this question of how experts who participate in a sharing network perform versus experts who make decisions alone, my colleagues and I conducted an experiment with 1,700 mid-career financial advisors. These are people who handle millions of dollars every day and work in financial centers around the globe. Networks of financial experts are a key example of a social institution that we depend on for the survival of our society because these same sorts of financial experts set tax policy, interest rates, and estimate the costs of social policies.

In one analysis by PhD student Dhaval Adjodah, we tested the performance and reliability of expert networks by asking financial experts to forecast the future price of various assets.[15] We gave them the opportunity to be part of a community consisting of all the experts so that they could see summaries of how other, similar experts were investing. In general, all the experts performed well (as one might expect for such highly trained and highly paid people). However, experts who were *not* swayed by what others were doing and made their decisions by relying only on data and historical models frequently did very slightly better than those who changed their investments based on what other experts were doing.

However, these independent experts, while more frequently making a bit more money, also more frequently made serious mistakes. Due to their mistakes, in the long run the experts who were completely quantitative and uninfluenced by the community of experts did *worse* than those who took the opinions of others into account. These mistakes were usually due to factors such as insufficient appreciation of the possibility of rare events or because they had not considered a wide enough range of possibilities (both are examples of the "Four Horsemen of Social Failure," discussed in the appendix). Historically, the only defense against these sorts of errors has been many minds and many opinions working to detect changes, to find exceptions from the general rule, to remind people about the possibility of rare events, and to try to notice new factors at play—all things that GenAI in particular appears to be good at doing.[16]

EVEN FOR EXPERTS, STORY SHARING IMPROVES INVESTMENT

The importance of being part of the expert community intelligence was nicely illustrated by one phase of our experiment, which spanned the period of Brexit when the United Kingdom left the European Union. During that period, we found that the isolated experts suffered big losses while the sharing-network experts did fairly well. From the point of view of long-term financial returns, the difference is huge: the very slightly better returns of the isolated experts were completely drowned by their mistaken Brexit investment strategy.

So, experts also need some sort of shared wisdom (referred to as "the street" in finance communities) to make reliably good decisions, not so differently from early humans sharing stories around a campfire. Even simple machine learning AI can provide feedback about what everyone else in the community is doing and thus help to improve decision-making.

TOOLS FOR SYNERGISTIC HUMAN-AI DECISION-MAKING

In this second half of the chapter, I will use the mathematical models described above to develop a taxonomy of digital tools that can help individuals decide what actions to take without removing human agency and judgment or preventing the development of social capital and trust.

In order for humans and digital technologies such as digital media and AI to be synergistic, they must support each other without unduly influencing each other. In other words, we are looking for technology that helps humans but does not remove human agency. We need to be careful about supporting but not replacing human decision-making and collective action mechanisms.

Our model of human decision-making tells us what needs to be done. Human agency originates from sharing stories, evaluating them, and using these stories to make decisions. These core processes—human learning, decision-making, and choosing actions—should not be manipulated by AI systems. However, human learning, decision-making, and action require support so that we can act successfully in our increasingly complex world. This support can be from social institutions (e.g., sharing stories around a campfire), the written word, or digital tools that help advance knowledge and communication but avoid persuasion. Obviously, the dividing line between knowledge, communication, and persuasion is both viewpoint dependent and uncertain, so we need to be especially vigilant about not building systems that veer into persuasion.

Human-decision support facilities can be separated into three main types:

1. The first type of digital support technology would be ways of collecting a portfolio of actions (e.g., behaviors and strategies) that the relevant community generally acknowledges to produce positive outcomes (forming the prior for individual decisions). Advisory services, or a digital search engine specialized for your various communities, are examples of this sort of decision support.
2. A second type of digital support technology would provide consensus information about the usefulness of a set of possible actions for people like you and in your situation. This information can help you evaluate your alternatives in the current context (forming the likelihood of positive reward given the individual's skills, knowledge, and context). Personalized data about health outcomes for various habits, financial returns for various investments, or career trajectories are examples of this sort of decision support.

3. A third type of digital support technology would focus on the resources for executing the action. Doctors and hospitals, investment services and banks, or job fairs are examples of these sorts of support facilities, as are community networking events, service organizations, and so on.

Each of these three categories of problems presents difficulties for human decision-makers, such as limited awareness of options or a restricted range of examples. Consequently, if well designed, each of these three categories present possibilities for digital technologies such as digital media and AI to help people without replacing human agency, and each has the potential to improve human community intelligence and shared wisdom. I will examine these three types of digital support technology in turn, and throughout the rest of the book they will be labeled *stories for ourselves*, *stories for me*, and *stories for change*.

DIGITAL SUPPORT TECHNOLOGY 1: STORIES FOR OURSELVES, OR WHAT DO PEOPLE IN MY COMMUNITY DO?

The core of this requirement is for everyone in a community to learn from the actions and results of others and to achieve consensus about which actions have the best expected reward. This is what this book refers to as shared wisdom, and it forms the basic prior probability model for individual actions within a community.

There are well-developed mathematical methods for doing this, but humans have significant memory and communication limitations. In addition, humans also have many competing needs and desires, so different people will interpret the utility of a reward in different ways, and the utility and reward will vary over time. The wisdom of the crowd is not a fixed set of rules or the same for all communities.

These limitations mean that human evaluation of potential actions will always be a very sparse data problem, and so it is essential to have methods of aggregation that combine experiences across long periods of time and across communities with similar needs and desires. In human societies this sort of large-scale aggregation has been served by myths, legends, and epic stories. The songlines of Australian Aboriginal peoples, the epic poems of Homer, and the myths of the Norse gods are all examples of this sort of aggregation.

Today's large language models (LLMs) can absorb these sorts of stories and then augment each individual's background intelligence. A serious problem with this is that the stories we have often come from eras with very different circumstances. For example, we now have medical, transportation, agricultural, manufacturing, and communication capabilities that are orders of magnitude better, and social roles (e.g., of women) that are dramatically different.

Today, web searches find stories that anyone anywhere has put online and that have proved popular in the recent past. Due to the popularity of this circa-2000 type of AI, search results are now heavily influenced by advertising and people with financial or political motives. Perhaps even more problematic, today's search engines personalize search results without regard to community or circumstance so that different people find different "truths" and are unaware that others do not share the same view of the online world.

Our understanding of human decision-making and the role of communities suggests that we need a different approach for AI-enabled search. Instead of a universal search engine or an individualized search engine, it makes more sense to have community search engines. For example, imagine that you could adjust the community you search within so that you could see what people in your neighborhood or in your profession or who share a hobby think about a particular issue. Obviously, privacy is a priority in such a search engine, but this is fairly easily solved using the same privacy mechanisms that are used in, for instance, creating census statistics.

Due to the importance of knowing consensus opinion within communities, members of our research network have designed and built AI prototypes to provide exactly this sort of private community search and community building. A collection of the relevant technologies can be found at https://transformers.mit.edu. The tools featured in this project site include not only privacy-preserving AI methods but also auditing tools, verification methods, and legal frameworks for safe and private AI. Chapters 4 and 6 will discuss how this type of community information is surprisingly effective at reducing political polarization and strengthening social institutions.

DIGITAL SUPPORT TECHNOLOGY 2: STORIES FOR ME, OR WHAT SHOULD I DO?

Just as important as knowing what actions generally work for people is to find what has worked well for people *like you*. This sort of question typically has even less data than the general "what actions do people typically take" question. To address this question, people use the answers to more general questions as a background prior probability to help evaluate the likelihood of success for the particular current problem and context.

As a consequence of this data sparsity, perhaps the main problem with answering "What do people like me do?" is finding "people like me." This is perhaps most obvious when considering problems like the management of rare diseases. Who else has this disease? What do they do that helps? Importantly, this same problem crops up everywhere. What colleges should I apply to given my grades, finances, and interests? What should I do about a boss that will not listen? Today it is quite difficult to find a set of people who have been in your exact situation, tried something, and reported about how it worked out.

Many of the earlier types of AI that have been deployed are intended to answer these sorts of questions in well-understood areas like physics, engineering, or finance. These AI tools are mostly focused on integrating data to make predictions. Examples are financial models for retirement and investment, weather models for everyday predictions or investigation of climate change, and optimization methods for planning vacations or scheduling package delivery. Because these sorts of technologies provide humans with capabilities that are clearly beyond what a single person can do themselves, they are generally designed to be advisory services and so tend not to diminish human agency. Even the best prediction tools can, of course, be used in problematic manners, that is, to set up systems that try to persuade or order people around or systems that act without human oversight.

In more complex areas, such as those involving human behavior, we have to use data from other people's experiences in order to make predictions or judgments. In the past this has typically meant census surveys or data collected from people's behavior (e.g., number of riders on a bus line, number of taxpayers), and more recently, data from online behavior (e.g., people's buying behavior or online search behavior). Today the ubiquity of harvesting online behavior data has become problematic because it has led to alarming concentrations of data and has created privacy concerns.

Fortunately, there are now cryptography methods that allow *private community discovery*, for example, finding other people "like me" without sharing who the other people are, and without sharing the information itself. That sounds impossible, but it is real and works efficiently. The key is that for a particular topic a person can encrypt data in a way that allows the computer (or phone, service, etc.) to detect when somebody else has encrypted data that seem similar. The user can then ask for introductions, and if that is successful, begin a conversation about mutual interests and concerns.[17]

Alternatively, a user can ask *privacy-preserving questions* about the entire community. For instance, "Do people with my disease also drink green tea, and does it seem to help?" And then, using similar sorts of cryptographic methods, that person can find out if green tea typically helps similar people.[18] The bottom line is that there is now private AI that serves community needs without ever sharing private data. The trade-off is that users have to be part of communities that share common concerns and participate by having their phones or computers answer privacy-preserving questions (i.e., questions that do not reveal the user's identity) about that concern for the benefit of the community. Prototype examples of these sorts of systems can be found at http://transformers.mit.edu, which also features auditing tools, verification methods, and legal frameworks for safe and private AI.

DIGITAL SUPPORT TECHNOLOGY 3: STORIES FOR CHANGE, OR HOW CAN WE WORK TOGETHER?

The final capability that we need our social institutions to provide is assistance for collective actions that are supported by consensus within the community. In today's societies, collective action is often left to legislators to craft policies and to bureaucracies to formulate and enforce regulations as well as to provide support and incentives for desired behaviors.

This method of collective action was originally designed during an era that was dominated by hereditary elites, and so perhaps it is no surprise that the system is famously resistant to change, lacks transparency, and is largely unaccountable. However, very recently researchers have developed privacy-preserving technologies to support collective action, and so technologies such as digital media and AI now have the potential to be an important supporting technology while not abridging human agency.[19]

There are at least two important aspects to consider in order to support collective actions. The first is creating methods of achieving consensus that are smarter, more inclusive, and more agile. I discuss this in some depth in chapters 4 and 6. The second is to create less rigid, more accountable social institutions to replace today's bureaucracies. An example of using *consensus networks* (discussed in chapters 4 and 7) to better support collective action is the volunteer not-for-profit Uniform Law Commission, which has been continually updating and harmonizing commercial and rights law across the United States since the late 1800s. This network, which is collaborative rather than hierarchical, accounts for about 10 percent of the laws enacted in the United States.

NEXT STEPS

The first half of this chapter examined how inclusive sharing of stories within a community enables much better decisions than reasoning things out as an individual. It also can build trust within the community, known as *bonding social capital* (defined, roughly, as willingness to help), and enable collective action. The second half of this chapter developed a taxonomy of digital tools that can be synergistic with human development of community intelligence and shared wisdom, supporting collective action without unduly influencing human agency.

Companies are already deploying early versions of each of the stories-for-ourselves, stories-for-me, and stories-for-change technologies. Today these first AI support systems are aimed mostly at business processes, helping with finances, hiring, marketing, and such. As outlined in chapter 8, we need global regulation that requires audit trails and liability enforcement in order to minimize, if not eliminate, problems like bias, unfairness, and lack of inclusion as these systems are rolled out.

But large corporations are also contemplating using AI support systems for radical structural change. For instance, stories-for-ourselves systems are anticipated to be useful in dealing with the loss of culture and context that plagues modern international corporations that have offices distributed around the globe and now have to deal with work-from-home arrangements. AI support systems could make distributed and work-from-home arrangements far more successful. Again, open audit trails and regulatory enforcement will be key.

Perhaps the most exciting direction is the creation of digital tools to help *personal* health, financial decisions, career choice, and many other areas we care about. The big consumer companies, not-for-profit organizations, and startups alike are already planning for a wide variety of personal support AI agents on mobile phones. Notably, Bill Gates is on record for thinking that the personal market for AI support tools is likely to be the biggest market for AI.[20]

The question, of course, is whether these personal tools will be free of centralized control or yet another way for large corporations and governments to influence citizens. The answer depends on who controls personal data, who makes the decisions, and how our social systems are regulated. These are the topics that will be discussed in the second part of this book.

3

BRIDGING NETWORKS AND INNOVATION: THE RISE OF CULTURAL WISDOM

The previous chapter examined how digital tools can help communities' story sharing produce the shared wisdom required for collective action without unduly influencing human agency. But what about stories from other communities? If a community has residents who interact with and learn from many different types of communities, then that community is more likely to prosper. These intercommunity connections are the social bridges along which new stories can flow. Modern examples of social bridges are sharing stories with people from different communities at work, while shopping, or just out enjoying recreational activities. The combination of all these social bridges is what I will call a *bridging network*.

Bridging networks matter because they give communities access to different pools of information and new opportunities, and they provide different perspectives. Interaction with culturally diverse communities increases people's ability to make use of new opportunities by giving them access to the ideas, skills, and tools required for productive activity and cultural adaptation. As a result, leading social scientists, such as Evans, Edward Glaeser, Ronald S. Burt, Michael Macy, Duncan Watts, David Lazer, Esteban Moro, Dino Pedreschi, and others, have shown how bridging networks create the scaffolding for bringing rapid innovation to our community intelligence and shared wisdom.[1] And as Glaeser of Harvard has emphasized, these sharing processes build social capital (roughly, willingness to help) and so not only improve community efficacy but also result in better outcomes on all fronts.[2]

In the first half of this chapter, I explore how bridging networks function and discuss how people have engineered cities to improve the effectiveness with which stories spread over social bridges. In the second half of this chapter, I will then explore the use of digital networks and AI to further improve bridging and thus accelerate the formation of community intelligence and shared wisdom.

STORIES OF THE PAST

In early hunter-gatherer societies, trading stories and tools and intermarriage with other communities were difficult due to the cost of travel and the danger of conflict. Early human societies invented the tradition of clan meetings and festivals probably because they made sharing stories, trading tools, and intermarriage much easier—until the food ran out. These intermingling opportunities, which are the forerunners of modern religious festivals and business conferences, were costly in terms of time, energy, and food but provided an important, albeit time limited, conduit for innovation.

Due to the cost of attending, it is likely that most groups attended infrequently, rather like the Muslim Hajj or Hindu Kumbh Mela today. The experience at such festival sites may well have inspired hunter-gatherer bands to seek ways to spend more time in proximity to other groups of people. It is likely not just a coincidence that the oldest known cities have been found in the same region as Göbekli Tepe in southeastern Turkey's Germuş mountains, where the oldest known festival site was created between 12,000 and 10,000 years ago.

However, life was hard in the early cities. Skeletons found at those sites are stunted and show the effects of hard labor, but because of this lifestyle innovation, more children survived and the population grew more quickly than in hunter-gatherer bands. Since that time, people have understood that intermingling with people from other communities is a reliable way to find new opportunities.

When neighborhoods are connected by social bridges so that their residents spend time together, whether at work or at play, they learn from each other and begin to adopt the most useful of the others' behaviors and attitudes, along with useful skills, knowledge, and social institutions. Interactions between members of different communities result in building a more diverse portfolio of community intelligence along with the social capital that enables larger-scale collective action. All of this can produce more effective institutional innovation.

It is clear that cities are engines of innovation and provide residents much greater access to new opportunities. Cities facilitate the human interactions and story sharing needed for good ideas and new opportunities to spread, and they sometimes transform society. So, even though cities are usually more cramped, expensive, dirty, and dangerous, the improved access to opportunity may be why people keep moving to cities and cities become larger and larger.[3] But is city size, with all the costs and associated problems, the only solution? The answer is no: There are other ways to make it easier for people in different communities to connect.

ENHANCING PHYSICAL BRIDGING NETWORKS

Knowing the bridging network between communities gives us a way to estimate the flow of stories between communities and to predict how changes in behavior will spread.[4] For instance, in a recent study that examined the spread of new behaviors within a large European city, we found that the bridging network structure was dramatically better at predicting the spread of a wide range of behaviors than were standard demographics such as age, gender, income, and education.[5]

The ability to predict the spread of behaviors and innovations has important implications for the management of public health, financial stability, and security. For instance, a large-scale study conducted during the COVID pandemic showed that pairs of cities with frequent population mobility between them (e.g., Boston and San Francisco, or New York City and Miami) exhibited more similar COVID vaccination behaviors than other cities of comparable size, even after controlling for political and economic similarities.[6]

By leveraging the bridges between differing communities, we can rather dramatically improve public policies. For instance, in a recent study members of my research network estimated the bridging network of the entire United States, and from that calculated the optimal COVID vaccination campaign. We discovered that the best strategy for vaccination was to focus on the bridges between vaccinated and unvaccinated populations, with the result that a 1 percent increase in vaccination rate resulted in a roughly 10 percent reduction in COVID cases.[7] Moreover, this bridge-focused strategy was more effective for minority and undervaccinated communities than simply focusing resources on them directly.

Bridges are also critical for resilience to disasters. The number and strength of connections between communities is called *bridging social capital* and it is a measure of how valuable different communities are to each other, and so it predicts how much effort they will invest in helping each other. Communities with lower bridging social capital have a harder time recovering after a disaster and are also less likely to have successful innovations.[8] Communities need the help and ideas of other communities in order to survive and thrive.

Government institutions are naturally beginning to take notice that using AI to leverage the pattern of bridging networks can make public services more effective. For instance, the Singapore government is supporting a large AI project with MIT, led by Jinhua Zheng, that will leverage their bridging patterns in order to both improve public health for seniors and provide more useful employment opportunities to workers.[9] Efforts to improve bridging networks within cities can have profound effects on all aspects of life, and so the following few sections will explore how bridging networks affect some of our most critical problems: how to raise successful children, increase societal wealth, decrease crime and poverty, and minimize the chances of intergroup feuds and war.

RAISING SUCCESSFUL CHILDREN

Recently a 20-year-long, whole-of-society experiment in the United States called the Future of Families and Child Wellbeing Study (FFCWS; formerly the Fragile Families Study) examined the development of 4,242 children, interviewing primary caregivers at birth and again when children were ages one, three, five, nine, and fifteen years, together with in-home assessments of the children.[10] The researchers also obtained large amounts of additional information on parents' medical, employment, and incarceration histories and their religion, childcare habits, and early childhood education. In total, 12,943 measurements were made of each child and their family, including scores on an extremely wide variety of standardized tests.

A total of 160 academic teams competed to use these data to predict the life outcomes of these children. My MIT team produced the most accurate models for half of the life outcome prediction tasks.[11] Despite the rich dataset and state-of-the-art statistical methods, our best predictions for these life outcomes were only slightly better than those from a simple benchmark consisting of separating children into bins by race, family income, and whether or not both parents were present.

The uncomfortable conclusion is that we cannot reliably predict children's life outcomes from any of the standard tests or interview methods applied to either the children or their families. These results point to a blind spot within Western society: We focus too much on the individual and not enough on the surrounding community.

In contrast to the FFCWS, the Opportunity Atlas study of the "American dream" of intergenerational mobility examined the effects of community. A group of Harvard and Brown University economists led by Raj Chetty and John Friedman obtained access to 30 years of longitudinal data from the US Internal Revenue Service.[12] From these data, they could compute the rate of intergenerational financial mobility across all US census blocks (i.e., neighborhoods of a few thousand people).

They found that the characteristics of the surrounding neighborhood mattered most; specifically, the exposure to opportunities and neighborhood social capital are both strongly dependent on a healthy bridging network. Shockingly, they found that approximately one-quarter of this neighborhood effect is "locked in" by the time a child enters kindergarten, and approximately half of the neighborhood effect is in place by the fifth grade. That effect size is about the same as is commonly attributed to the genes inherited from a child's parents. In other words, a child's life outcome is mostly locked in before they reach puberty.

SOCIETAL WEALTH AND INNOVATION

As discussed in the last chapter, it is instructive to analyze how communities build wealth. Building wealth is a clear, measurable goal, and because many people are interested in building wealth, it is a good laboratory for understanding how community behavior promotes or hinders desirable outcomes.

Wealth creation is, of course, a complex, dynamic feedback process with no one causal factor. Greater diversity in the network of communities that interact does result in greater income on average—this is the idea of weak ties bringing new opportunities—but it is also true that greater wealth causes social networks to be more diverse because it becomes easier to find and leverage new ideas and opportunities. So instead of asking what causes prosperity, as if prosperity were the outcome of some simple machine-like process, it is better to instead ask how much influence each factor (e.g., community intelligence, capital, education, bridging network, etc.) has on the whole cycle of wealth creation. The important question is not what causes wealth creation but which factors are the most influential in creating wealth.

Our experiments examining the bridging networks within cities on several different continents demonstrate that access to diverse communities is one of the most important elements of the wealth generation process.[13] For example, when we examined over 300 cities in the United States and European Union, we found an extremely strong relationship between how well the transportation network connected different communities within a city and the rate of wealth creation across the whole city.[14] Enhancing a community's intelligence by drawing from the experiences and skills of other communities is an extremely powerful driver of wealth creation.

However, the most effective bridges are to communities that are just a little bit better off than your community. Evidence from social media, for instance LinkedIn, suggests that the connections that are most effective at improving life outcomes are connections to people that are moderately wealthier.[15] In other words, to help the lowest-income communities, the most useful connections are to communities that are one rung higher on the socioeconomic ladder.

The idea of promoting bridges between low-income communities and those that are just a bit wealthier is also behind a project to create coworking spaces in underused Boston libraries. MIT PhD student Nicholas Caros found that five of the potential locations straddled the border between a very low-income neighborhood and a working-class neighborhood. They calculated that selecting these sites for coworking spaces would provide greater benefit to the city than putting the coworking spaces in more homogeneous areas of the city.[16]

Another method of improving bridging networks is to extend tax breaks to stores that produce more mixing between communities. Investment in a city's bridging network need not be expensive. For instance, research led by Moro has shown that streets with lots of coffee shops and street food, where people gather and talk, are not only extremely good mixing places but also help the neighborhoods they serve to increase their wealth, and they even reduce crime in the area.[17]

This research quantifies an intuition gained over the last few centuries, namely that coffeehouses and informal food stalls are a nexus of story sharing that enables cultural change. This idea goes back many centuries, and sometimes governments have even tried to suppress coffeehouses because of their capacity to bring together different communities to share ideas and opportunities and thus enable collective action and change. For example, in 1675, King Charles II banned coffeehouses throughout England, but political pressure forced him to back down quickly. So far, every attempt to ban coffee has eventually failed.[18]

A related example of the effectiveness of bridging in promoting innovation comes from our study of 3,555 business incubators in China. When we surveyed thousands of startup enterprises in China, we found that diversity of cultures (e.g., having experience in different cultures, or having lived in different countries) and diversity of skills (e.g., having school training in different fields) were two of the most important factors for predicting company success.[19]

Many avenues of evidence support the idea that increased connectivity causes increased wealth, and the studies described above suggest that investing in a city's bridging network is one of the best ways a city can prosper. The observation that bridging networks significantly predict such disparate areas as financial growth and child development suggests that conventional factors—investment, education, infrastructure, institutions, and so on—may not be direct causes of improvement. Instead, these factors may make a difference primarily because they either help or hinder the ability to build a more diverse network, search for new opportunities, and then exploit those opportunities.

POVERTY AND CRIME

That a community's bridging network is so important for the development of children and for economic development suggests that social bridges play a critical role in persistent poverty and crime. Data from cities around the world show that people who live in one neighborhood typically work and shop in only a few other neighborhoods. Consequently, there may be only a small number of strong social bridges between their home neighborhood and other neighborhoods.[20]

Moreover, severely disadvantaged neighborhoods frequently lack new opportunities because their social bridges often only reach other severely disadvantaged neighborhoods. For instance, Robert Sampson at Harvard has used cell phone data to show that severely disadvantaged neighborhoods in Chicago have almost no connections to differing parts of society and so have fewer social bridges to bring in new ideas or opportunities. In this regard, these neighborhoods are almost as isolated as physical ghettos. Isolated neighborhoods such as these are, unsurprisingly, the worst off out of all communities in a city.[21]

Not only does the extent of their isolation predict their crime rate but, as the Opportunity Atlas studies showed, these are the conditions that result in poor life outcomes for children. One remedy is to leverage AI methods to help design smarter cities with better bridging networks. AI research has already shown that it can help us imagine designs that provide better connections to diverse communities and provide underserved communities greater access to opportunities.

POLARIZATION: THE PATH TO WAR

Trust is central to most social functions and is especially important for democratic deliberation and collective action. For instance, citizens in a democracy must be willing to trust both that compromises are fair and that others are not cheating. Lack of trust provides would-be authoritarians with a powerful weapon because by stoking fears about potential opponents' commitment to fair dealing, they can seize greater power and gain acceptance of undemocratic and even unethical behaviors.

In a recent paper led by PhD student Alia Braley and with collaborators from UC Berkeley and MIT, we called this predicament the "subversion dilemma" because it has parallels to the "security dilemma" that is central to the realist view of international relations.[22] In the realist view of how wars develop, fear incentivizes state A to arm itself against potential attackers. State B is likely to interpret this military buildup as a potential threat and increase its own military spending. State A then reacts in kind. This cycle may continue until one state decides to preemptively attack rather than risk annihilation. The result is that warfare breaks out even though everyone prefers to avoid the costs of war.

Similarly, escalating fear between partisan groups can lead to increasing perceptions of threat. The ability to weaponize the fear of others is a key part of a larger set of mutually reinforcing polarizations, including heightened partisan identity strength, heightened dislike among partisans, and increased dehumanization among partisans.[23]

In our subversion dilemma paper, we found that when people knew more about the intentions of the other side, they had more trust that everyone was abiding by democratic norms and they more frequently voted for democracy-promoting candidates. This result parallels research in international relations on the security dilemma, which also suggests that tools such as third-party observation of behaviors that signal partisan intentions, along with costly signals of good-faith intentions, are possible ways to resolve such dilemmas.

This idea that mutual knowledge, especially knowledge about intentions, improved trust among partisans was further tested in a recent megastudy, led by Robb Willer, by recruiting 32,059 subjects to test 25 interventions designed by leading academics and practitioners.[24] Interventions that corrected misperceptions about the intentions of opposing partisans were among the most effective in increasing support for democratic practices. Because the online testing environment of this megastudy resembled typical online environments, we would expect similar effects for participants who engaged with the interventions on these sites. For example, this study found that a short, gamified question-and-answer session about the intentions of opposing partisans led to a significant reduction in misperceptions and increased support for democratic policies.

BRIDGING VERSUS BONDING

Learning from and working with diverse other communities is a critical part of building a thriving society. Communities that have only a few bridges or only bridges to very similar communities gain little from those interactions and so have limited opportunities to learn new behaviors or skills. On the other hand, strong ties within communities are critical for integrating new ideas and opportunities into their institutions and for giving communities the resilience to overcome challenges and the agility to take advantage of opportunities.

Each person and each community has a limited amount of time and energy to connect with other people, so we must balance building connections within our community (increasing our bonding capital) with building social bridges outside of our community (increasing our bridging capital). Our social institutions and physical infrastructure either facilitate or hinder these two types of social capital building.

People tend to trade off bridging and bonding capital by focusing on bridging when the future is uncertain and on bonding when the environment seems stable. New ideas are critical to survive in uncertain times, and collective actions are critical to capitalizing on opportunities when times are good. This trade-off is known as the exploitation-exploration dilemma, and it highlights the need for sharing ideas and opportunities both within and between communities. It is also exactly what is predicted by the minimum-regret model of social learning that was discussed in chapter 2. The trade-off between bridging and bonding explains why communities that are cut off from the rest of society by social or physical barriers, as well as communities without strong community cohesion, have such a hard time thriving.[25]

Interestingly, high school children seem to intuitively know that connecting different communities is an important part of success: Children from disadvantaged communities have about 50 percent more "aspirational" friends (e.g., the popular "cool kids") than do children from more average communities.[26] In fact, one unforeseen problem with busing children from low-income communities to schools in high-income communities is that the bused-in children often have little opportunity to form friendships with children from other backgrounds because the bused-in students arrive at the start of school and leave immediately at the end. Evidence from several sources shows that it is the pattern of friendships, and not the curriculum, that has the strongest effect on academic performance.[27]

It is important to realize that the lack of social bridges between low-income communities and wealthier communities is not simply the result of historical patterns of residential segregation. In fact, the majority of experienced segregation is actually caused by cultural patterns that reinforce racial and economic segregation where we work, shop, and play.[28] Even small, unarticulated differences in how people are treated can deliver the message of "you don't belong here."

The evidence suggests that the main driver of segregation is that many of us feel uncomfortable with people different from ourselves. Consequently, behavioral and cultural barriers in day-to-day interactions are likely the major barrier to bringing opportunities and ideas into the community. In other words, cultural conventions and social institutions that limit social bridges between communities may be the major source of failing children, poverty, and crime. Using AI visualization methods to better understand these cultural problems seems likely to be a productive research area.

SYNERGISTIC DIGITAL SUPPORT FOR BRIDGING

In the second half of this chapter, I examine how digital networks and AI could improve bridging between communities. Digital social networks were originally promoted as a major improvement in our ability to find new friends and relationships and in giving voice and access to everyone. Unfortunately, many have turned out to be echo chambers that promote anxiety and distract from developing trusted relationships and building social capital. Digital social networks are a classic example of technologies that fail to appreciate the complexity of human life and so suffer from unintended consequences.

A major part of the problem is that digital social networks are typically dominated by a few loud, attention-grabbing voices (called "dragons" in some academic disciplines), and as a result, many digital social networks appear more like a collection of cults than a reasonable and collaborative society. Even worse is that virtually all media platforms—social media and traditional media alike—are managed by maximizing cash flow from ads and purchases and consequently seek to monopolize our attention.

They profit from promoting loud, adrenaline-producing voices and provoking a good fight.

While these problems are most visible in digital media, the same dynamic exists in almost every industry that uses digital networks to engage with their customers. Unlike earlier industries where income was proportional to the number of customers or amount of production, today's data platforms encourage rich-get-richer exponential growth that makes markets intrinsically unstable and vulnerable to domination by a few data-rich corporations. When a company knows a great deal about its customers, it can tailor ads and offers specifically for each person. By leveraging our online behavior, it is able to distort our decision processes to its advantage.

So, what does the fact that influencers and data-rich companies tend to get even richer mean in the real world? As demonstrated in our *Proceedings of the National Academy of Science* paper, the mathematics of the network effect means that in a market where a dragon has already emerged, removing it from the network severs only one of the many heads of the rich-get-richer hydra, and inevitably a new dragon will appear to take its place.[29] To slay the beast, the underlying system-wide distribution of data power must be balanced, thus creating a healthier, more competitive system.

SLAYING DRAGONS

We have given digital media, and commercial enterprise in general, special privileges in our society because they play a crucial role in creating the common good. The evidence is that their digital business models are causing unintended but important problems, and so they need to do a better job at fulfilling their side of the bargain. The core problem is driven by the fact that harvesting people's data creates a dynamic where influencers, political organizations, and marketing corporations expand their messaging until they dominate our limited attentional resources. Consequently, a good way to restore productive civic discussion and improve community intelligence is to change the incentives for data acquisition so that the rich-get-richer dynamic becomes muted.

In the case of digital media, for instance, if we simply taxed people with more than 10,000 followers as a business using a common resource, digital media would not have such a problematic role in society. People confuse "free delivery" with "freedom of speech" despite the fact that TV stations have always had to buy licenses, cell phone companies have to buy wireless spectrum, and magazines pay for postal delivery. Businesses have always paid to use the public commons, so why shouldn't digital media?

The same feedback loop—the data dragon problem—also occurs with the systems that feed, clothe, govern, pay, entertain, and educate us. Taxing or regulating businesses by the number of customers or amount of data would also help with the data dragon problem and would dramatically improve antitrust regulation.[30]

However, such a progressive tax scheme addresses only part of the issue. For instance, it would still miss the problem that digital businesses are almost always centralizing forces as well, applying uniform rules to very different communities, resulting in bias, unfair practices, and discouraging inclusion. To address this problem, it is best to think about giving more control to communities rather than just improving the way that stories are shared. Data cooperatives are the solution many countries are pursuing (as seen in the recent G20 meetings); and in the United States, public service organizations such as Consumer Union (better known for their Consumer Reports) are introducing helpful solutions.[31] For instance, my research group has worked with Consumer Union to create an online facility called Permission Slip, which gives people much greater control over their data by leveraging California privacy law, and we are now working with them to develop and field individually owned AI agents that act as "consumer champions." These personally owned AI agents can act as fiduciary agents on your behalf the way that doctors and lawyers do by helping to navigate the complexity of legal agreements, commerce, and government systems.

STORIES FOR OURSELVES: BUILDING AI FOR COMMUNITIES

Many of the studies discussed in this book show that physical copresence typically drives both personal access to opportunities and accumulation of social capital. This may be part of why people in cities typically move many kilometers per day, traversing several different physical neighborhoods. They also go to many different shops, buy food, and use public spaces almost every day.

However, it is also true that good decisions require story sharing from people with similar concerns and circumstances. So, while the typical person is around many other people, it is difficult to know who you should talk to and about what. It turns out that the pattern of where you go and where you spend your time is a remarkably good reflection of your interests and can be used to find people with shared interests. The problem with using these sorts of data to help you meet interesting and useful people is that they are extremely sensitive and private.

It is potentially important, therefore, that modern cryptography has made it possible to find people with similar interests without endangering users' privacy. We can now have consent-first, private information sharing to drive social feeds from users' personal private data, specifically using mobility traces on their phones, but without the data ever leaving the phones.[32]

This privacy-preserving technology designs the feed to explicitly optimize for integrating the user into the local community by encouraging activities that bring you physically close to people with similar interests and concerns. This approach to promoting social bridges has several important advantages. First, it preserves personal privacy. Second, it makes dragons unlikely because the ranking mechanism makes it hard to promote oneself beyond just physically networking more. This limits the possibility of dominant agents emerging.

This approach to building a social feed can also reinforce and strengthen existing ties between people and communities by making it easier to reach people with shared interests and eliminating overly dominant voices. Because any echo chamber effect is connected to physical-world interactions, our traditional methods of managing conversational diversity continue to work. If you don't enjoy a particular club or store, you can just stop going there.

The change from talking to everyone in the world to talking primarily to people who share your concerns, situation, and values means that the dialogue is more likely to result in productive collective action. It is important to note, though, that the social learning process that enables consensus and collective action among community members is the same process that creates echo chambers. In the context of solving communities' shared problems, however, social learning could be a feature and not a bug.

NEXT STEPS: FROM BRIDGING TO SHARED WISDOM

In the next chapter, I examine the cultural invention of consensus networks. The consensus network process "mines" the stories that make up a community intelligence in order to obtain a set of stories that constitute a broadly shared wisdom and thus enable cooperative action. Consensus networks begin with the stories provided by community and bridging networks, but they also generate consensus on which stories are most useful by utilizing individual comments and an incentive mechanism to promote compromise among diverse populations.

The second half of this book, beginning in part II, explores previous deployments of AI in shaping our contemporary society and how AI can be used to improve our social institutions while remaining human centered, safe, and ethical. As with all AI-enhanced systems, open audit trails and regulatory enforcement will be required to minimize problems such as bias, unfairness, and lack of inclusion. This is the focus of the final chapter.

4

CONSENSUS NETWORKS AND COLLECTIVE ACTION: MODERN WISDOM AND SCIENCE

In the previous chapters of this book, I described two ancient cultural inventions: one that promotes story sharing within groups to create a community intelligence and shared wisdom that can dramatically enhance group decision-making, and a second that promotes story sharing among different groups to create a community-of-communities intelligence that dramatically raises rates of innovation.

The first half of this chapter will begin by recounting how these ancient social innovations depended on physical proximity. Writing and accounting ledgers were developed to improve memory and story-transmission quality, allowing for organizations larger than single cities, but these tools were historically restricted to members of the elite and their assistants. This suggests that at least until the beginning of the Enlightenment, the tools of writing and accounting were primarily used to extend the reach of central authorities rather than to broaden participation in decision-making or to raise the rate of innovation.

With the broader literacy of the industrial era and the proliferation of post offices and telegrams, the middle class could begin to leverage these modes of expression. However, it wasn't until the advent of the internet-enabled mobile phone that most people in the world could potentially participate. The question, of course, is how to leverage this new inclusivity for better institutions.

STORIES OF THE PAST: SCALING INSTITUTIONS

A central driver for the invention of new ways to share stories is the desire to overcome the limitations of existing systems. Human society developed during times when practical considerations such as the difficulty of travel meant that coordination among larger groups, such as clans, could ordinarily be conducted only through discussions among *representatives* from each tribe. The dependence on representatives limits the rate of story sharing and biases it toward stories that the representatives prefer. Historically, these tendencies have made it likely that a social hierarchy will emerge. Examples include many democracies, from the Athenian democracy to the members of today's parliaments and congresses, where representatives are typically drawn from the most educated and wealthiest strata of society. The emergence of elites is such an old problem that 2800 years ago the Greek philosopher Plato referred to it as the "Noble Lie."

Throughout the last several hundred years, many countries have moved to broaden the base of people involved in shaping society, often for practical reasons rather than ethical ones. In a world where a nation's wealth and stability depend on warriors, merchants, and bankers, it makes practical sense to include their stories in decision-making.

A well-known example of this process was the Hanseatic League, a coalition of as many as 200 communities in northern Europe, which dominated trade from the thirteenth to the seventeenth century. As merchants grew rich from trade, royalty accommodated power sharing with them because enhancing trade left everyone better off. In the 1700s the idea that the merchants and wealthy commoners should be part of the decision-making elite spread widely. In Britain this took the form of strengthening the House of Commons, while in America the founders gave all landowners voting rights. Traditional elites still mostly ran the show, but with these changes successful entrepreneurs could join in shaping law and regulation.

Similarly, the modern history of China illustrates this dynamic. Rule by Chairman Mao and the Communist Party was not very successful economically. After Mao died, the party allowed entrepreneurs to create businesses, and soon the economy boomed. In time, these wealthy entrepreneurs were encouraged to join the Communist Party. Today, of course, entrepreneurs are being forcefully reminded that the party's goals are paramount.

Despite efforts to broaden voter participation beyond the wealthy and hereditary elite, almost all democratic countries are de facto run by elites, usually employing occasional votes by "the people" to legitimize their rule, much like what was done in Roman times. Consequently, representative democracy and governance by a ruling class are often not as different as we would like to believe.

A story that highlights the similarity between governance by a hereditary elite and representative democracy concerns the founding of Japan's democratic government in the late 1800s. This story comes from a Noh play that I saw performed at Japan's state-supported National Theatre. The play's story describes Japan's transition from feudalism to a modern, democratic, capitalist society, and, according to my Japanese friends, it is intended to highlight the arrogance of Western societies and the ability of Japanese leaders to see the truth.

The story begins in 1870s Japan, when powerful warlords felt that Europeans were treating them like barbarians; this frustrated them in part because they saw European governments, including British and American democracies, as simply being the government of rich families and thus fundamentally the same as their feudal system. To fix this problem, they simply renamed everything. Their fiefdoms were relabeled "companies" and their serfs became "lifetime employees." Their first sons became presidents of the family company, and the second sons became members of the national parliament. As a result, Japan became recognized as a representative democracy, even though nothing had really changed.

ATTEMPTS AT SCALING COMMUNITY INTELLIGENCE

The ability to make reliably good decisions depends on being able to understand the experiences and goals of everyone else in your community. If decision-makers cannot learn from a sufficiently diverse and representative set of people within their community, then they cannot make the most broadly beneficial choices. In communities of up to a few thousand people, a determined individual can plausibly develop a good idea of what most everyone else thinks and feels and then integrate that information into their own opinions.

The problem that has prevented society-wide decision-making is the inability to scale the storytelling institutions originally invented for groups and cities. To accomplish this task requires transmitting stories across long distances without depending on either the sort of frequent physical interaction that enables transmission of a rich variety of stories within communities or reliance on a small group of representatives.

Perhaps the oldest method for achieving diffusion of stories and consequent innovation without having everyone talk to everyone else is to limit participation to a small number of more-or-less ordinary people and have them meet for a fairly short period of time. Historically this is the logic behind regional religious gatherings and festivals. Today this logic motivates business and scientific conferences, where typically there is a process to select good stories from each community and then have the stories' authors meet for a few days, share their stories, and then return home to spread the best of the stories they heard while meeting.

The fact that there is a huge, worldwide industry supporting these sorts of conferences and meetings is evidence that these multigroup storytelling sessions do indeed promote innovation and understanding within worldwide professional communities. They scale the sort of bridging network mechanisms that power urban innovation, but they are costly due to travel expenses, and they are dependent on the assumption that participants will successfully transmit important stories from the meeting throughout their home communities.

More recently the COVID pandemic provided a huge natural experiment in using video (e.g., Zoom, Microsoft Teams) to bring people together with much less cost and difficulty. The data from that experience are very clear: People can use video to work with people they know well, but much of the cross-community interaction that generates innovation is lost.[1] People are mostly traveling again, although hybrid schemes that mix going to the office with video-supported remote work are becoming the new standard. It seems necessary to maintain some physical proximity in order to promote cross-community innovation.

The visit-and-return-home idea is also the logic behind the representative form of government that was envisioned by some of the creators of the US Constitution. They imagined that representatives would still be part of their home community; that is, they would not live full time in the capital but would maintain farms and families in their home communities and would serve as representatives for only a few years. Since the founding of America, however, population growth has meant that political districts have too many people to really get to know firsthand what people think, and the advantages of living in the capital have meant that representatives live there more than their home district. As a consequence, the social bridges between individual community members and their representatives have thinned. Representatives are now members of an elite management class, and surveys show that citizens no longer trust them to understand their communities' problems and aspirations or to have their communities' best interests at heart.

Diminished ties between community and elected representatives have led to interest in an invention known as citizen assemblies that combine the logic of the US founders with the practice of modern conferences. In this approach to society-wide decision-making, citizens are randomly selected to meet and deliberate on current issues, and if enough people participate one can hope to get a good representation of the views of every reasonably sized community.

This approach has many of the strengths and weaknesses of public surveys because the assembly's governance—including discussion leaders, report writers, and even the general topics to be discussed—is usually managed by the government's professional bureaucracy. Furthermore, the outcomes of these assemblies are almost always advisory in nature, to be interpreted by those same central bureaucracies. As a result, while they are a useful new institution, they fail to address the problems of inclusivity and management by a professional elite.

CENTRALIZATION VERSUS INCLUSIVE GOVERNANCE

The dominance of individual leaders in today's social institutions is partially a legacy of the mechanical model of society. The seventeenth- and eighteenth-century concept of society as a giant machine leads naturally to letting the subject experts (i.e., politicians and academics) decide social policy. It is not accidental that this same time period saw the rapid growth of educational institutions for training young people to become elite professionals, awarding them degrees certifying that they can be trusted leaders because they *have been taught what to do*. All of this ignores situational change, personal temperament, and alignment with community values. Delegation of power is a convenient solution to the problem of managing social institutions in large, populous administrative regions, but it produces a hierarchy where centralized authorities tell citizens how to behave.

When power is held by a small group of people, they often end up making decisions that favor themselves instead of everyone else. This is not always outright corruption; rather it is more commonly regulatory capture, where the laws and regulations favor the decision-makers more than others. The World Bank estimates that damage to the world economy stemming from these regulatory capture problems runs from 5 percent of world GDP up to 20 percent.[2] Centralized systems generally make it easier for decision-makers to become wealthy, and this may be one of the main reasons that the adoption of distributed, more adaptable systems has been so slow.

There are also other explanations as to why we still have such centralized, top-down government, businesses, and social organizations. One reason is that it is faster and easier to let someone else decide. Our journalistic traditions reinforce this tendency by making leaders seem glamorous. In the popular imagination, the success of science, technological innovation, and new types of business is generally attributed to individuals and the training or support they receive. The role of their communities in these successes generally receives short shrift, in part because the individuals being highlighted by the press like being bathed in glory, and the news outlets make money selling such memorable stories.

Perhaps more important but less obvious is that the habit of delegating power is ingrained within all of us. It is the universal human experience of being a child and having older, taller people with lower-toned voices (your parents and teachers) always knowing what to do and physically enforcing rules. Even as adults, taller people and people with lower-toned voices make considerably more money and are more likely to be managers.[3]

So, how can we have successful, innovative societies without depending on a small, centralized group of decision-makers? Can we improve the range of people involved in governance so that we can better minimize risk from the Four Horsemen of Social Failure (unseen change, rare events, one-size-fits-none, and myopia, all described in the appendix)? The evidence, surprisingly, is that we can have good decision-making in law, public spending, innovation, and more without centralization and elites.

Beyond the institutions of storytelling in workgroups and bridging networks in cities, there is a third example of a naturally evolving institution for sharing stories that may make direct, inclusive democracy possible. During the last several centuries some widely distributed communities with common interests have developed a potential solution to having more inclusive and representative institutions: consensus networks.

We already have worldwide consensus networks, and they are cooperative, moderated storytelling networks (for example, scientific literature) that have shown they can reliably produce innovative stories that consistently help the whole society. These systems are exactly the sort of innovation engines that we need to address the global challenges that face our societies.

CONSENSUS NETWORKS: INCLUSIVE COMMUNITY INTELLIGENCE OVER SPACE AND TIME

The idea of widely separated individual people sharing stories and building on each other's work emerged as a force for innovation during the seventeenth century. The term "men of letters" first appeared in the early 1600s (and they were indeed almost all men) as individuals began to write and share physical letters about what they called natural philosophy. Their shared goal was to build a more systematic understanding of the physical, biological, and social worlds. There is a good argument that it was this new institution of trading letters that produced the flowering of science and culture known as the Enlightenment.

These informal communities of inquiry were systematized beginning with the founding in 1665 of the *Philosophical Transactions of the Royal Society* and the French *Académie des sciences*. These first scientific journals did something that had rarely, if ever, been done before: organizing the thought of many individuals by requiring citations to other works and comparing new work with that of other people. This generated an easily accessible consensus network that allowed people to determine who was interested in which ideas and what they thought of each idea, but without the need for a central authority.[4] The power of a consensus network is not that everyone comes together in a consensus but rather that it allows a clear and relatively unbiased view of where there is emerging agreement and where there is division. Consensus networks therefore enable an understanding of the evolution of community opinion and the emergence of agreement.

Previously, libraries like that at Alexandria had been created, but they were not generally accessible and neither did they organize the pattern of discussions among different viewpoints. Theological debates, such as which books should become part of the Christian Bible and which new ideas should become part of Christian theology, were similar, but rather than being unrestricted discussions they were strictly controlled by central authorities such as the Roman pope or Byzantine emperor. Perhaps closer to the invention of scientific journals is the development of the Talmud, but this ancient consensus network has been almost entirely concerned with religious philosophy and practice and also has an intentionally limited audience.

INCENTIVES FOR CONSENSUS

The institution of citing and analyzing each other's work in print included one other absolutely essential social innovation: incentives for consensus. The authors of papers that had many citations and were much discussed often received appointments to serve as professors and were sometimes given lucrative royal appointments. They could even be elevated to membership in a new branch of aristocracy, becoming a fellow of the Royal Society and similar institutions.

These perks provided a strong incentive to produce works that yielded consensus among the contributing authors and so become part of the scientific, political, or engineering canon, analogous to religious canon, allowing the authors to accrue some measure of fame and fortune. The same incentive mechanisms still exist today, with tenured university appointments dependent on citation count and success in obtaining research grants, consulting income, or lecturing fees all closely related to the number of citations on topics with broad interest.

BUILDING CONSENSUS NETWORKS

The idea of using citations of earlier work to organize the thoughts and research of many people has proven truly revolutionary and is now central in academic inquiry as well as in technology development (e.g., patents) and common law (used in about one-third of all countries). Its key innovative properties are that (1) people are not limited by physical distance or selected by a central authority and are instead free to find a community with shared interests; (2) by publicly linking and comparing their contribution to others, participants establish a reputation within the community and build social capital with authors of work that they approve of; and (3) the existence of strong incentives for authors to produce content that generates consensus. The citation network continuously organizes individuals' thoughts into communities of interest and forms bonds between members of the community. The result is a platform for trading stories over long distances that also preserves the ability to establish a reputation and build the social capital that can concretely benefit the individual.

Citation networks have recently drawn considerable attention because of their importance to scientific progress, and questions abound about why some papers get so many more citations than others. Is this due to the author's reputation? Is it biased? Do topics fade over time? How do scientists' career trajectories and citations of their papers relate to each other? The recently published *The Science of Science* by Dashun Wang and Lazlo Barabási collects their extensive work on this topic and shows that analysis of individuals and growth rate in citation networks can provide deep insights into the process of scientific discovery and similar domains.[5]

THE STRUCTURE OF CONSENSUS NETWORKS

The evolution of consensus, however, depends at least as much on the community interested in a particular issue as on the participants and stories themselves. To explore the role of community in consensus networks, PhD students Sadamori Kojaku and Robert Mahari, guided by faculty members Sandro Lera, Y. Y. Ahn, Esteban Moro, and myself, used sophisticated mathematical embedding methods to analyze citation patterns and found that in three very different domains—science, patents, and law—the community-based innovation mechanism that drives progress is very similar to the minimum-regret decision-making that drives investment decisions among eToro's financial traders.[6] Scientists, entrepreneurs, and judges are all hunter-gatherers in their different story-sharing domains.

For science, patents, and law, the process of searching for stories that form new connections within a community with common interests is a surprisingly good method of predicting what topics will become "hot." Similarly, predicting who is likely to participate in the community thinking about this new topic depends on their connections to the new story. An important insight is that instead of a story's popularity being solely due to characteristics of the story itself or its author, popularity is *mostly* due to consensus within the community of shared interests defined by the network of citations. The popularity of certain stories in science, patents, and law, as measured by their citation count, illustrates the mechanism whereby new ideas are added to the collective community intelligence.

Part of the genius of this naturally evolving citation mechanism is that it does not define community based on fixed features like nationality, gender, or age, and there is no central authority judging people's work. Instead, success depends on whether other people interested in the topic think your contributions are appealing enough to link to via a citation in papers that they write. Consequently, the self-defined community comes to a consensus by a convergence of interest.

It is rather shocking that the same process drives the evolution of ideas in domains as different as science, patents, and law. In science, anyone can join, and success is defined in part by the number of citations your work attracts. In patents, anyone can file, but success has to do with profitable business ideas and citations show the breadth of applications enabled by your invention. Citations in law, however, come from a highly structured system. Citations are generated from legal decisions by judges in court cases that are randomly assigned to them. Moreover, there is often a hierarchy of judges (supreme, federal, and local courts), so different types of judges get different sorts of cases. In law, the incentive for consensus is reputation: When a legal decision has lots of citations, that means that it is literally precedent-setting—creating common law—and is seen as a badge of honor for the judge.

Even though the details about how scientific papers, technology patents, or legal decisions are generated are quite different, it is surprising that none of these details affect the dynamics of how these three very different communities have evolved over time. This suggests that the dynamics of these three domains are processes for evolving a community's intelligence that depend on human interest and attention together with the incentives for consensus, not on other features of the author, the story itself, or the network.

PREDICTING INNOVATION

One of the most interesting things about being able to use mathematical embedding techniques to predict hot topics is that the evolution of consensus within a community is surprisingly predictable *without* examining the content. Instead, simply by estimating the community's focus of attention as inferred from the citations between contributions, one can tell years in advance which topics will attract the greatest scientific interest, the greatest business interest, and the greatest amount of legal activity.

We cannot use this sort of embedding technique to predict exactly what the most important scientific finding will be, or what the most profitable new patented technology will look like, or what the most contentious legal decision will be. But now for the first time we do know where to look. Some venture capitalists are already applying similar techniques to guide their investments, and the peer review process used in science funding agencies provides the sort of incentive mechanism that reinforces the consensus process.[7]

It is worth asking if social institutions like government should be using this predictive analysis of consensus networks to set policy. For instance, if one scientific story is hot but there is no patent activity in the area, should funding institutions begin to include money for more practical applications of this new idea? Or if an area is seeing lots of new patent activity but also lots of legal debate, should that be an area that draws regulators' attention? Innovation funding that has the advantage of knowing the consensus around the science, technology, and legal questions is likely to be more productive and consistent with social values.

I think the answer is that the use of mathematical techniques for predicting areas of innovation has obvious advantages for accelerating innovation and also obvious dangers for misallocation of society's resources. This question is very much like the general question of where to invest: One must spread investment and risk across many strategies in order to have a good likelihood of success. Consequently, allocating some resources to areas that are predicted to be hot makes sense, but it does not make sense to dedicate all of the resources to predictions from this one AI method. One advantage of treating AI prediction tools this way is that they do not replace human judgment or agency but rather complement human intelligence.

DIGITALLY ENABLED CONSENSUS NETWORKS

The previous sections of this chapter discussed the relationship between the structure of consensus networks and innovation. In this section I address the question of whether consensus networks and technologies such as digital media and AI can be used to manage social institutions. Two of the most important properties of consensus networks are that they are scalable and that they are not constrained by physical proximity. Some of these networks include millions of people across every country on earth, and since the late 1700s we have been using this new cultural invention to guide progress in science, health, and more. This is truly a cultural invention that has potential for wiser, more inclusive governance of entire societies.

So, what is the evidence for how best to use consensus networks to manage and improve our social institutions? Let us look at three examples: one in medical science, one in technology development, and one in law.

A striking example of a consensus network is found in scientific efforts to improve public health practices. During the last few decades, informal networks of doctors and nurses sharing data about innovative infant care practices have dramatically improved health care for babies, reducing death rates by an order of magnitude. These improvements usually begin with local groups that experiment with new methods and then share their experiences with others in journals and, more recently, in open repositories like arXiv. The incentive mechanism comes from society's recognition that they have helped alleviate human suffering. This recognition also helps contributors' careers and allows them to obtain more support from central funding agencies. As the story about a successful new health intervention attracts attention, it spreads to other locations, and then central financial support can begin to make the new intervention widely available to others.[8]

In the field of technology development, a familiar example is open-source software, which is computer software created by communities of interest and made openly available to anyone who wants to use it. Many of our basic digital technology systems and standards have been created by experts who volunteer their time to help improve the systems that seem most interesting to them. They discuss ideas with each other, trade code and whitepapers proposing different protocols, and meet together. When there is convergence of opinion, then consensus protocols (usually including example computer code) are included in the world's digital commons. The incentive for contributors is recognition and the greater likelihood of career advancement, not too different from the incentives in science and medical research.[9]

In the field of law, an example of this type of consensus network is the Uniform Law Commission, established in the United States in 1893. It is a not-for-profit network of lawyers supported by contributions from all 50 US states who come together to discuss how laws affect outcomes across all states. By examining problems shared by states in domains such as trade, residency, social services, and so on, this consensus network connects many communities and tries to find ways to harmonize interactions between them.

To do this, they perform a meta-study of the experiments running in each state to reach a consensus on best practices in areas ranging from commerce to tax policy to child adoption to treatment of mental illness. The incentive for the participating lawyers is knowing that they have contributed to the public good, recognition by peers, and a greater likelihood of a successful law practice.

Importantly, these legal scholars and their recommendations do not create law or set regulations. Instead, each state legislature considers their recommendations, and if a legislative body agrees, it enacts a law based on the recommendations but often with variations to account for local conditions. This process of measuring, learning, and adapting accounts for about 10 percent of changes to all US laws, and it is why commerce works across state lines and allows people to move between states relatively painlessly.[10]

As can be inferred from these examples, the consensus network systems we have today are most often used to guide more centralized systems for funding, legislation, or setting bureaucratic priorities. They are almost never free of some type of central control. In chapters 6 and 7, I describe how to use consensus networks to enable more direct democracy and potentially much more agile, effective governance. I also describe how AI can potentially be harnessed to improve humanity's community shared wisdom—and how it could lead us astray.

NEXT STEPS

During the eighteenth and nineteenth centuries, the Western world was building centralized institutions in line with the mechanical model of society, while more organic, agile institutions based on consensus networks quietly emerged out of the spotlight. These consensus network institutions drove an explosion in scientific knowledge, a revolution in manufacturing and medicine, and the governance of it all by the case-by-case decisions that make up common law. The hope is that we can build social institutions based on these types of consensus networks instead of centralized, hierarchical bureaucracies.

How might we best use modern digital tools and new AI capabilities to create more inclusive and effective government without compromising human agency, introducing bias, or hindering inclusive participation? Digital media can potentially remove some of the practical constraints of our existing institutions and permit much greater scaling. AI and digital media together may also have the potential to help make large-group decision-making more inclusive, efficient, and effective. But obviously these same digital tools could be used for yet more centralization and repression of new ideas and behaviors.

In the second half of this book, I examine how to use technologies such as digital media and AI to better support our social institutions and government without reducing human agency or resorting to top-down, uniform rules. This will hopefully provide insights into how to best use these technologies to build more human-centered and agile social institutions. Finally, I discuss approaches to regulation and global cooperation that can create social institutions that are safely and effectively enhanced by digital media and AI.

II

How digital systems can support human social processes to build better social institutions.

5

UNINTENDED SIDE EFFECTS

The first half of this book outlined how storytelling networks, bridging networks, and consensus networks provide the basis for our community intelligence, innovation, shared wisdom, and collective action. I have also described how our current institutions are failing us. The question for the second half of this book is, How can we leverage digital media and AI to move from the current situation to much more agile, innovative institutions that better serve us all?

To begin to answer this question, this chapter starts by describing the three previous AI boom-and-bust cycles and finding commonalities that may help society leverage the capabilities of AI while avoiding problems in the current and future AI booms. Rather than seek fixes for current problems such as bias or lack of inclusivity, the goal will be to discover principles that will minimize these problems in the future.

This is a rather daunting task, worthy of a book or two in its own right, so it is worth mentioning that the AI stories and observations presented here have an unusual, close-up perspective due to my having taught at MIT with some of the creators of AI, including Marvin Minsky and Geoffrey Hinton (at Woods Hole), and many other leaders in the field. Similarly, observations about the societal effects of AI reflect the perspectives of national and international political leaders as seen during my work with EU leaders to kickstart the General Data Protection Regulation (GDPR; the EU privacy law), my work with the UN Secretary General's office as a "data revolutionary" helping to shape the Sustainable Development Goals, and discussions with the former prime ministers and presidents of EU nations within the Club de Madrid during their early discussions about regulating AI.

As context for this chapter, we should remember that technologies for sharing stories, finding consensus, and taking collective action have a checkered history. For instance, the invention of the printing press led to less expensive books, but it also enabled an avalanche of pamphlets—pamphlets such as Martin Luther's 95 Theses, which ignited the Protestant Revolution and led directly to a century of war in Europe. More recently, radio and TV have homogenized our collective intelligence and shared wisdom, raising concerns about the destruction of traditional and local cultures and causing ill effects in children. These modern technologies have also reinforced the power of the state and wealthy corporations, thereby disenfranchising minorities and impoverished groups. Although digital social media were initially hailed as a restoration of the voices of these minorities, these newest media have caused a splintering of our shared wisdom into echo chambers and fostered worries about unforeseen effects on children that are similar to the worries that accompanied the introduction of radio and TV.

Perhaps most relevant for our future is the rise of digital technologies such as mainframe computers, PCs, cellphones, and the internet. During the 1950s, as the first digital computers became available, these technologies inspired researchers to see if intelligence could be explained in terms of computation, and the field of artificial intelligence began. AI was seen as potentially improving society's intelligence by providing an alternative to the weaknesses of human reason and deliberation.

Unlike earlier technologies of writing, accounting, and printing, which each improved our ability to remember and communicate stories, AI's goal was to discover new, possibly better stories by combining analysis and data. From the beginning, people were both fascinated and fearful of AI, much as they were with stories of artificial humans like the Golem or Frankenstein's monster.

In fact, the founders of AI selected the name for exactly that reason: It was a name that was sure to stimulate research interest and obtain funding from the government. It has been clear since the beginning that AI would likely automate certain jobs, even though it would make other jobs easier or more productive. More worrisome is the possibility of putting too much trust or authority in AI decisions and having that cause a disaster.

THE EFFECTS OF EARLIER AI ON SOCIETY

The field of AI has had several periods of intense interest and investment ("AI booms") followed by disillusionment and lack of support ("AI winters"). Each cycle has lasted roughly 20 years, or one generation. The important thing to notice is that even though these earlier AI booms are typically viewed as failures because they did not create a big new AI industry, below the surface each AI advance actually exerted enormous effects on commerce, government, and society generally, but usually under a different label and as part of larger management and prediction systems.

AI IN 1960: LOGIC AND OPTIMAL RESOURCE ALLOCATION

The very first AI systems were built in the 1950s, and most were formulated on the idea that intelligence can be captured by logic and mathematics. They were primarily deductive reasoning systems that attempted to duplicate the sort of logic that goes into mathematical proofs, or the sort of math that calculates the shortest route for a delivery truck to take or how to pack items into a truck. There was also a thread of research aimed at understanding biological intelligence, and this thread would eventually form the basis for the AI of the 2020s. These various threads soon separated and became known as logic, cybernetic, and neural network systems.

The logic and mathematics systems generated enormous excitement because solving logic and math problems is so hard for people and, at the same time, so important for economic efficiency. The early systems worked shockingly well for these sorts of problems, saving companies a great deal of money. Today, software packages that do these sorts of calculations are built into everything from spreadsheets to industrial production systems to dating apps and are thought to be among the most common types of calculations done everywhere across the world.

Other AI systems first built in the 1950s were based on neural networks, which are a very simplified model of how neurons in the brain connect and pass signals to each other. These models were originally intended for research into how the connectivity of brain cells produced intelligent action but had limited practical applications due to inadequate computer hardware. However, these early models slowly got better as computers got faster, and today modern versions of these early neural networks power the deep learning networks on which the AI of the 2020s is built. It just took 70 years.

UNINTENDED SIDE EFFECTS

These early AI methods were very successful at well-defined problems like proofs or optimization, and they have also been widely used for predictions in more complex domains such as economics and climatology by use of abstract models of these areas. Indeed, the US Congress requires the Office of Management and Budget to predict the cost of new legislation, and the International Panel on Climate Change uses this 1960s, mathematical type of AI to forecast climate change.

However, as might be expected, some people tried to apply the AI methods that worked so well on smaller problems to manage society at large, originally under the banner of "optimal resource allocation." In 1959 Leonid Kantorovich published his book *Best Use of Economic Resources* and the Soviet Union began to manage its economy using his system. Despite this research winning a Nobel Prize in Economics, the Soviet Union's experiment in optimal allocation of resources was a disaster that contributed to its eventual dissolution.

THE FOUR HORSEMEN OF SOCIAL FAILURE

The problem that the Soviets had was not so much that the AI failed; rather, the fault lay with the models of society they had available. Those models failed to capture the complexity or dynamism of society and also suffered from problems like misinformation, bias, and lack of inclusion. As has occurred so often in past history, thinking of human society like a big, predictable machine doomed this ambitious effort. Today we have much more complex models of society, but they still fail to capture the unexpected changes and chaotic processes that give rise to innovation and crashes and that drive the continuous evolution of cultural norms.

These same problems can be seen in quite recent examples of today's digital media and AI systems again going badly wrong. In fact, these same mistakes happen so frequently that I call them the Four Horsemen of Social Failure (for more, see the appendix). An example of the first horseman, *unseen change*, is found in the collapse of Silicon Valley Bank in 2023. In this case, rumors on social media were a major cause of a digital run on the bank: The spread of digital media, together with the immediacy of digital funds transfer, meant that rumors of a bank problem could cause coordinated movements of big depositors. Unfortunately, this sort of instant run on a bank was something banking regulators had never thought about. The second horseman, *gray swans* (rare but unavoidable events), appeared in the 2008 financial crash when supposedly safe financial instruments failed to account for the possibility of simultaneous spikes in mortgage defaults in almost every major city. The third horseman, *one-size-fits-none policymaking*, emerges when the government creates a policy that suits the majority of communities but hurts minority and disadvantaged communities. For instance, the smaller or newer members of the European Union famously suffer from policies that help Germany and France. The final horseman, *myopia*, appears when policymakers neglect important factors, such as those found in today's high-speed stock market trading. These trading platforms suffer market crashes almost daily because the algorithms fail to take into account the possibility of liquidity constraints.

AI IN 1980: EXPERT SYSTEMS

In reaction to the limitations of the first AI systems, researchers began to look at *expert systems*, which replaced the rigidity of logic and numerical solutions with the heuristics that human experts had developed to solve each type of problem. These systems aimed to apply human rules rather than economic laws to data in applications where it was too difficult or expensive to have a person do the work.

For instance, one of the early applications was ordering all the brackets, wires, and connectors needed to install complex electronic equipment. People could do the job, but they often ordered the wrong parts or left something out, and the cost of hiring a specialist to help made the cost of the equipment too high. Consequently, this was a good place to use an expert system to automate the ordering process.

The early successes of expert systems with small problems suggested to senior managers that they might be able to tackle larger problems. For example, one of the major problems in consumer banking has always been how to make good loans. In the 1980s each bank branch, credit union, and loan association had neighborhood offices where credit managers would assess people's creditworthiness and decide whether they should grant a loan. This was a huge labor cost, and loan quality varied from credit manager to credit manager. Moreover, recent antidiscrimination laws made banks liable for lawsuits when credit managers were prejudiced against protected people or communities. The obvious solution was to automate the task by using expert systems to obtain consistent loan rules everywhere across the country.

UNINTENDED SIDE EFFECTS

This application of expert systems to bank loans sounds like a good idea, but there were important and unintended side effects.[1] Replacing decisions made by people familiar with the community with a central expert system AI meant greater uniformity of the loan process, but the specifics of the community were no longer taken into account. The systems reinforced existing biases and limited inclusivity.

Perhaps even worse was the hollowing out of communities. Loan officers disappeared, as did credit unions and cooperatives. Branch offices of large banks held on for a while but quickly became mostly ATM locations and deposit windows. The resulting concentration of data and financial capital led to more than half of the community financial institutions in the United States disappearing over the next decades. Today, as shown in figure 5.1, these sorts of local institutions are largely gone.

From the 1980s onward, AI technologies such as expert systems have been built into virtually all digital management systems but described using phrases such as "business intelligence" or "enterprise management systems." Like the 1960s wave of AI technology, expert systems are so common today that we often forget they were once cutting-edge AI. Many factors contributed to the society-wide collapse of community institutions, but one of the biggest and least appreciated factors was this second wave of AI.

As a consequence of the ubiquitous deployment of this AI technology, this same process of centralization has led to the disappearance of

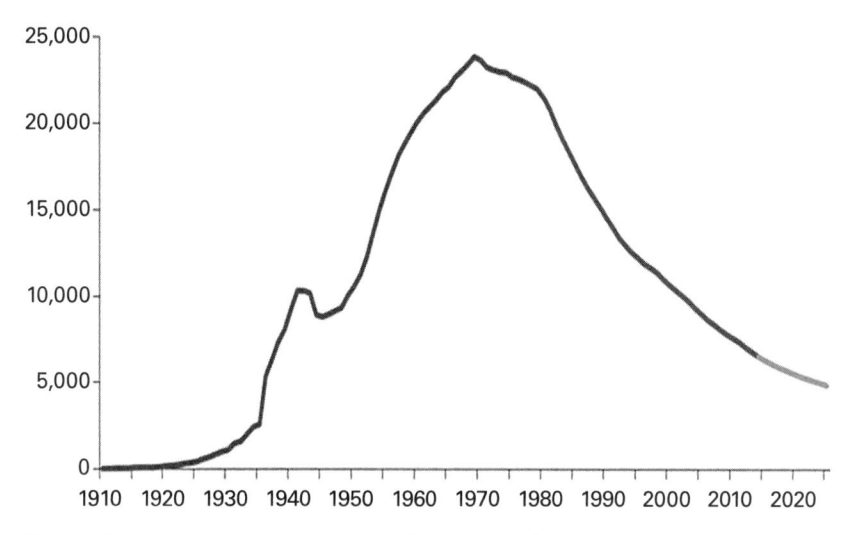

Figure 5.1 Number of community credit unions in the United States: actual (1910–2014) and projected (2015–2025). *Source*: Redrawn from Luis G. Dopico, *Credit Unions: Financial Sustainability and Scale*, Report #401, Filene, April 19, 2016, https://www.filene.org/reports/credit-unions-financial-sustainability-and-scale.

local hospitals and neighborhood governments. Moreover, as local governments, clinics, and credit unions disappeared, communities found they had no one to ask about how to go about getting help and no one who would bend the rules to help cases that did not quite fit the official stereotypes.

INNOVATION DIMINISHED

Similarly, in 1980 the majority of workers were employed by small businesses serving mostly one community but by 2010 the majority were employed by big businesses with national or international agendas. This shift to centralization was reflected in stock market valuations, where the biggest companies grew the fastest.

A significant consequence of the loss of community-based institutions is the loss of community control and citizen engagement. Centralization also impacts innovation because small, young businesses are generally more nimble and innovative than big companies. In 1980, 12.5 percent of companies were less than a year old, but by 2014 this number had shrunk to 8 percent—and this shift likely contributed to the overall slowing of economic growth and the rise of inequality as the creation of new, small companies slowed and business moved to big cities where there were more technology-savvy workers.

COMPLEXITY

Centralization has another more subtle but hugely corrosive effect: as larger systems are forced to account for unusual edge cases, they inevitably become more complex, harder to manage, slower to adapt, and therefore (ironically for a "cost-savings" technology) much more expensive to change. For instance, software systems for small businesses (e.g., QuickBooks) that are simple, cheap, and robust turn into hugely expensive custom systems, like the enterprise resource planning vendor SAP, when stretched to cover a multitude of localities and products. Similarly, legal systems that are typically simple, robust, and understandable (e.g., local sales tax) turn into nightmares of complexity and cost when stretched to cover an entire country (like the United States' Internal Revenue Service Code). The complexity and expense that come with centralized systems benefit the government bureaucracies and software management behemoths such as Oracle and SAP but leave citizens lost in increasingly complex systems.

AI IN THE 2000s: HERE BE DRAGONS

In the last part of the 1990s there was a huge economic bubble as businesses moved en masse onto the internet. Amid all the hype around fiber optic cables and digital switches, there was a less frequently noted explosion of data about users and their buying patterns. Every time someone did something on the internet, those data were recorded by the seller, the platform, the banks, the credit scoring agencies, and more.

Researchers and entrepreneurs began to notice that they could target individuals for offers or ads based on their previous behavior and on the behavior of similar people. It is this process of understanding users by their data, originally called "collaborative filtering," that powered the rise of Google, Facebook, and similar digital giants and resulted in what is now called "surveillance capitalism."[2]

Much has been written about the dangers of data being concentrated in the hands of a few powerful organizations, and I myself worked hard in the 2000s to co-lead discussions at the World Economic Forum (WEF; known popularly as Davos) that produced the EU privacy regulation GDPR, one of the few large-scale bulwarks against misuse of personal data.[3]

UNINTENDED SIDE EFFECTS

Less discussed but perhaps even worse was that the collaborative filtering process meant that people would be preferentially introduced to ideas that similar people enjoyed, resulting in echo chambers. This propagated existing biases, misinformation, and other problems.

Even more dangerous is that people would be shown content and made offers similar to that which had drawn the attention of people like themselves, a process called "preferential attachment." So not only do "people-like-me" collaborative filtering algorithms produce echo chambers, but they also make it likely that the echo chambers will be dominated by a few voices that are unusually good at grabbing people's attention. These attention grabbers become disproportionately loud voices that accumulate very large audiences, and their dominance undermines the possibility of balanced civic discussions where all voices are heard.

The socioeconomics literature has named these dominant voices *dragons*.[4] In ancient cultures, dragons were seen as powerful and capricious agents that could overwhelm everything else. Today's dragons are similarly powerful and capricious but very much real: They are agents that overwhelmingly dominate our media, commerce, finance, and elections. By dominating attention and gatekeeping conversations, they are perhaps the ultimate examples of how to surreptitiously control markets and public debate, undermining democracy as well as lawmaking and regulation.

The problem with the dragons that dominate our digital media is that their ability to constantly grab user attention creates a powerful feedback loop, a rich-get-richer process in which the loudest voices grow the fastest, eventually dominating popular attention so much that they crowd out everyone else's voice. The reason this happens is that humans are not isolated individuals; instead, we constantly learn from each other and make decisions based on others' experiences through face-to-face networks, social media, and all the other networks that connect us. Memes, fads, and panics often start when an overly dominant voice spams many people with the same story. The contacts of the people receiving the story are then likely to hear about it and join in the conversation. Then the friends of friends join, and the conversation snowballs to include everyone.

These sorts of rich-get-richer communication patterns are called *preferential attachment networks* because people preferentially start to follow more popular people. Preferential attachment networks exist not only in digital media but also in advertising and commerce. The consequence is that only a few actors end up with large audiences and large amounts of data. When this sort of exponential growth is possible, some of these data-rich companies will grow into "dragons" that disproportionately dominate their audience's attention. In fact, the mathematics of social networks show that when data access is extremely unequal, it is inevitable that dragons will arise to dominate everything, *and that removing today's dragons simply clears the way for new dragons*. In this situation, traditional antitrust methods will not limit the rise of dragons—the only solution is to decrease the level of inequality.[5]

Today, our public life and culture are dominated by dragons, and they drown out other ideas and voices and thus prevent collective rationality and block collective action. If these dragons were the voice of reason and public service this might be acceptable, but instead too often they are attention-seeking politicians, entertainment stars, and ad campaigns hyping new products with the hope of creating a profitable new fad.

With some changes to our current systems, it is possible to have the advantages of a digital society without enabling loud voices, companies, or state actors to overly influence individual and community behavior. Concrete suggestions about how to regulate the data economy to best maintain the principles of human autonomy, privacy, and fairness were presented in chapter 3 and will be elaborated later in this chapter and in chapter 8.

AI IN THE 2020s

Today we have AI in most of our phones and cars and in retail and commercial systems. We use it all the time and love it. These earlier AI systems work reliably well in part because they are almost all employed as methods to manage specific human organizational functions: shipping, payments, wayfinding, and so forth. They present projections based on simulations but do not directly change what people believe or how they act. However, companies and governments too often present these simulations as "the truth," frequently picking models that are biased to support their interests.

The technology behind today's AI is quickly evolving to become cheaper, more energy efficient, and ubiquitous. It will be everywhere, just like previous waves of AI. While public attention is focused on LLMs like ChatGPT, many uses of the new wave of AI are not based on text but instead on other sorts of data. Like previous waves of AI, these data-driven prediction systems will also be used for a wide range of specific problems—for example, prediction of protein folding, weather, finance, and health, to name a few.

The current wave of GenAI differs from the last waves of AI, however, because it can tell stories and draw pictures. It mimics human intelligence by collecting our online stories and imagery and, when prompted, playing back combinations of them to us. These AI systems are built not from facts, numbers, or syllogisms but rather from the sort of stories that humans have posted online in order to think about and guide behavior. This reliance on people's digital commentary makes GenAI prone to the propagation of biases, misinformation, and more.

The AI of 2020 does not "think" any more than the previous generations of AI did. Yann LeCun, one of the creators of today's AI and head of Meta's AI group, relays an amusing story of how the best AIs of 2024 failed with the following problem-solving challenge: A man and a sheep stand by the edge of a river with a boat that can hold one man and one sheep. How can they get to the other side of the river? The best AIs could not answer the question because no human had ever written down the answer to such a simple question.[6]

Since humans choose actions based on the stories they believe, and the collective action of communities depends on their consensus stories, the effect of GenAI telling stories in response to our questions can have much more of a direct impact on what people believe and how they act. In contrast to earlier waves of AI, GenAI can not only project likely outcomes but will also directly recommend actions to take based on a mishmash of stories it has seen. The actions these AI systems produce will certainly include those that cause unintended effects and may include others that completely remove human agency.

The fact that humans can and do natively digest stories to build community intelligence and guide collective action gives this wave of AI a worrisome power to influence people that earlier AI technologies never had. At the same time, this new AI is currently weaker at reasoning than even the 1960s AI technologies.

LESSONS FROM THE PAST

What can we learn from these earlier deployments of AI? Where are they most likely to go wrong? I think that there are four main areas where there could likely be significant negative consequences, but also opportunities for positive outcomes.

DATA OWNERSHIP AND PRIVACY

The first area concerns privacy and the control of data. Earlier waves of AI did not directly address the matters of privacy or data ownership at all. People and organizations have to share data in order to get appropriate services and answers, but this sharing has traditionally been modulated by trust, community, and the need to preserve individual reputation. The importance of this topic is why I co-led WEF discussions on the topic starting in 2008.

Control of data is not just for privacy or for breaking rich-get-richer feedback loops but also for security and safety. As we become more and more digital, issues of systematic digital fraud and potential cyberattacks by state actors need to be given serious attention. The fundamental elements of ensuring safety are through control, provenance, and audit trails to ensure that the streams of data that manage our society uphold the standards we expect and need (see chapter 8 for a more detailed discussion).

In order to have AI systems work well with humans and our institutions, we need to incorporate data ownership rights as part of AI's fundamental architecture. For example, today if you are interested in buying a car and visit a car information website, everything you do is tracked and then sold to car dealerships as a sales lead. It ought to be possible to search for data about cars without being tracked, and in fact some websites, such as Consumer Reports, allow you to do just that. Consumer Reports also offers a facility that my research group and I helped design, called Permission Slip, that gives consumers the ability to have personal data control on other websites by leveraging the California Consumer Privacy Act.

AI IGNORES HUMAN COMMUNITIES

A closely related area concerns the fact that all of the earlier waves of AI either ignored personal characteristics completely, treating people as if they were interchangeable gears in some big machine, or data about each person were used to analyze their individual tendencies, often by comparison to people with similar tendencies. The fact that people make decisions by leveraging the intelligence of their different communities has been ignored completely.

For instance, Google originally gave everyone exactly the same answer about which web pages were most connected. Everyone was treated as if they had the same concerns and interests. Later, Google introduced personalization, which biased the search results based on your previous searches, using data from other people with similar patterns of search. But this ignored the importance of community. The best answers for you depend not only on the particular topic and your personal circumstances but also on the opinions of people who share your interest in the topic and whom you trust to help you understand the problem.

As an example, imagine you or a family member have a rare disease. Using a search engine to find treatments that could help will often yield paid advertisements and opinion pieces from people who may or may not be qualified or trustworthy. Moreover, your searches will make you the target of ads for all sorts of questionable products and services. There ought to be a trustworthy facility for finding out what people who have the same problem are doing, and your search should be private. In fact, there is a website like this, called PatientsLikeMe.com, which is wonderful but handles only serious diseases like Alzheimer's or ALS. A more general tool for finding and sharing anonymized community information is what I call *stories for ourselves*, and it is a prime opportunity for community-aware AI.

DATA OWNERSHIP GIVES DISPROPORTIONATE POWER

Every wave of AI depends on digital data, typically collected through digital channels, and this unfettered access to personal data has been used to manage the spread of information and stories in social, financial, organizational, and consensus networks. Unlike the storytelling networks that create community intelligence, which until recently depended on face-to-face conversation or the printed word, almost all digital networks have rich-get-richer feedback loops.

This feedback loop makes popular bloggers more likely to grow even more popular, gives well-known commercial brands a greater chance of dominating their market, and helps drive centralized, uniform management of services. The consequence is that our choices and our discussions are dominated by only a few alternatives, which is a recipe for poor decisions, panics, and crashes. We need story sharing that invites us to consider a wider range of alternatives and enables humans to make better choices.

Moving toward a more diverse ecosystem of stories and ideas, one that can enable better decisions, can only be achieved by greater equality of voice, as shown in our recent paper in *Proceedings of the National Academy of Science*.[7] This can be achieved by dampening the rich-get-richer feedback loop through means such as a progressive tax on the number of followers on social media or the number of customers a business has data on combined with antitrust action based on data ownership rather than market share.[8] (These ideas have been discussed more thoroughly in chapter 3.)

IRRESPONSIBLE AI

As AI technologies have spread and been built into everything, they have brought greater efficiency and organization to the world. Despite worries about AI overlords, AI has not replaced human agency as the primary driver of innovation and community intelligence. However, AI technology has caused significant problems, including bias, unfairness, and lack of inclusion, mostly through network effects caused by *how* they were deployed.

For instance, today the vast majority of AI applications are currently used for prediction. Companies and governments pay attention to these projections, of course, and change operations and policies on the assumption that the projections are more or less accurate. Unfortunately, the past waves of AI brought changes to the way our systems work and so caused problems such as centralization of decision-making, concentrated data ownership, and the creation of echo chambers as previously discussed. The AI itself was not the problem; rather it was the way that managers and politicians misused the AI's projections that caused these unintended effects on our social institutions and our ability to control our lives.

Most of these problems are caused by AI being deployed without the contextual feedback and built-in circuit breakers needed to avoid problems such as the devastation of community efficacy and trust caused by the centralization of financial, medical, and governance institutions. Many of these unintended side effects are the result of business leaders and policymakers treating people as independent individuals rather than as members of communities who learn from and depend on one another. Failures caused by ignoring damage to the person-to-person connections that drive a community's intelligence require constant monitoring if we are to detect and mitigate them before they do too much damage.

As discussed in chapter 2 of this book, it is best to think of people as being able to be collectively rational but typically not individually rational. People are not just individual actors; they are part of their communities' collective actions. Policies and systems designed for independent individuals often fail because they do not work for the community, or they damage the connections between communities.

ETHICAL PRINCIPLES FOR AI

What does all this tell us about where to deploy this new AI, and where to use caution? In a recent whitepaper I coauthored with Lily Tsai and our students on this subject, we offered a framework for how to think about designing prodemocratic uses of generative AI, assess the opportunities and risks of current technologies in terms of this framework, and identify the most promising directions for integrating generative AI to support online discussion and deliberation.

The four principles of this framework are that GenAI should (1) assist people without reducing their agency; (2) treat all people as equals and enable people to treat each other with mutual respect; (3) protect people from harm by biased algorithms or bad actors while engendering the trust essential for participation in democratic deliberation; and (4) abstain from holding office and not serve as our representatives in policy deliberation or collective actions.

This framework suggests that we should focus today's AI in the same way we use our other storytelling mechanisms (e.g., as a resource to support human storytelling, innovation, and consensus networks) instead of having it directly provide answers or make choices for us. As Adam Smith might have suggested, we should focus AI technology on connecting us to each other and helping with the sharing of favors and ideas instead of using the mechanisms of competition and markets.

There is always the temptation to let AI systems make decisions for us rather than be limited to aiding human decision-making. This temptation comes from the belief that we have all the facts and theories that we need in order to logically plan out our entire society. This belief is pure hubris because our world not only changes constantly but also continues to experience rare, large-scale, but unanticipated events. Further, the long-term effects of our choices are inherently nearly impossible to predict (see the appendix). All animals, humans included, have inherited a collection of quirks, biases, and tendencies formed by a billion years of evolution. We are very far from understanding how these apparently illogical characteristics may or may not have been critical to survival in our uncertain, chaotic world. We must avoid the hubris of believing we can logically plan for everything, or that our rules are eternal.

NEXT STEPS: BUILDING SOCIAL SYSTEMS THAT LEVERAGE AI

Ethical principles are important, but how they are implemented is at least as important. How can we focus AI, and GenAI in particular, to help society and avoid unintended consequences? In chapter 2, I explained how human decision-making and collective action can be divided into three main components:

1. Sharing stories about what actions people similar to you take, and what results they had, in order to learn the most useful actions. This is often called social influence or social learning and builds community intelligence. The process of trading stories is a type of sharing that helps build bonding social capital.
2. Sharing stories with different sorts of people in order to discover new methods and strategies of action. This is often referred to as the effect of weak ties. The process of trading stories across different communities helps build bridging social capital.
3. Achieving consensus within communities on what actions are most useful and which actions will be most useful in the future. This is how the shared wisdom of a community, when combined with social capital, enables collective action.

These three sorts of "community AI" can be harnessed to support a wide range of human activity within social institutions—for example, to find out what others are doing, what is typical for people to do in your current situation, or what is the best strategy for you in particular. They are also domains where we must be vigilant about bias and misinformation. The next few chapters explore how we can use these three types of digital support systems to build governance systems that have synergies between AI systems and human society while minimizing problems such as bias and misinformation.

Chapter 6 examines the possibilities for digital democracy to inform policy. Often, we think of democracy as voting for representatives who will decide policy and manage the bureaucracies that carry out policy. But legislatures and bureaucracies are slow to change, often too self-interested, and disconnected from the lives of most people. This chapter will go on to explore the use of more inclusive and accountable methods for governance. There are already well-proven consensus networks that provide a more grassroots and inclusive method of deciding policy in many aspects of our society (e.g., the commercial code, medical treatment, etc.), and these consensus network methods need to be applied to a much wider range of problems.

Chapter 7 focuses on the problem of designing bureaucracies that are agile, flexible, and responsive enough that they can be counted on to benefit society as originally intended. I will review the Ostrom principles for successful governance, which require that governance structures are able to carry out policy in ways customized to each community. Today there are a few examples of large government agencies that leverage digital media and AI to be more agile and effective, and these examples of best practices need to be adopted more broadly.

Finally, chapter 8 addresses AI regulation that provides practical methods for beginning to correct problems such as bias and lack of inclusion. This chapter will also consider how we can build a common regulatory framework among nations so that we can avoid the problems of regulatory arbitrage. Unless we have compatibility of AI regulation among nations, AI services will inevitably migrate to the least regulated jurisdictions.

6

REINVENTING DEMOCRACY

In this chapter and the next, I outline where we need to go in order to have the sorts of governments we want, and I discuss the beginnings that are already in place. This chapter focuses on democracy, which I define as building and harnessing the shared wisdom of an entire society with the goal of creating better policy. The following chapter focuses on implementing policy by replacing today's clunky bureaucracies with more agile and inclusive social institutions. The final chapter, then, proposes a regulatory approach that can give us safer, more useful AI and enforcement through global cooperation.

STORIES OF THE PAST

For millions of years, humans and our earlier hominid forebears were social species that lived in groups of no more than a few hundred individuals. Our dependence on social learning and how this creates community norms of behavior is literally in our DNA; it is the motivation for storytelling and the scaffolding for the development of our community intelligence.

Only two hundred years ago, more than 90 percent of humanity still lived in such small groups. Even today, across all countries and cultures, we organize our lives around small groups of friends and coworkers, and it is the cultural norms of these groups that determine most of our behavior. Perhaps the most obvious element of culture is that the attitudes and behaviors of each individual are similar to the attitudes and behaviors of the people that they regularly interact with; in other words, culture is built on shared norms and values gleaned from our community.

Nevertheless, as the human population grew and we moved into densely packed cities, the support provided to individual decision-making by community norms began to become less effective. The search for shared wisdom became much more difficult because we found ourselves drifting in oceans of strangers. For instance, it is estimated that only 3 percent of our conversations are with neighbors. Our cultural reinforcement mechanisms became diluted because there were fewer consistent behavioral norms to guide us toward successful cooperative behaviors.

To compensate for this dilution of local norms, over time we adopted more and more complex institutions to patch us together and to coordinate our (limited) individual capabilities. The social learning mechanisms that humanity evolved for cultural adaptation were replaced by bureaucratic rules and regulations, and society became managed by a greatly expanded professional class. Often these changes to central management increased efficiency, but they also disenfranchised citizens and made society less able to adapt to local conditions.

The advent of digital systems and earlier versions of AI have dramatically accelerated the trend toward centralization of our institutions. In addition, they have enabled dominance by big companies and bureaucracies that hold data about enormous numbers of people. This has pushed us beyond what our current institutions can handle, leaving us with diminished community ties and less effective institutions.

To address these problems, we first need to step back and use better scientific tools to gain a clearer understanding of human nature and the structure of our societies. One of the key aspects of forging a better understanding is to go beyond the rational individual and society-as-machine thinking from the Enlightenment and Victorian periods to a more modern, scientific understanding of human nature and societal dynamics. These venerable models of human behavior and cultural change shaped the foundations of both our society's institutions and our thinking about our institutions, but they are now failing.

DIGITAL DELIBERATION

How can our multimillion-person communities and societies discuss what actions to take? Most physical communities are too large to fit in a town hall, and for communities of common interest there is no realistic possibility of getting together frequently enough to really manage their common concerns. We must look to new sorts of digital technologies instead.

This idea seems to have led to the creation of some of the first digital social media (e.g., The Well), which were intended to allow for creative and deliberative conversations.[1] Despite the excitement these early platforms generated, such a platform could not be successful for solving community-wide problems unless a large fraction of the citizens utilized it for deliberation about the problems facing their community and debates about alternative actions with serious intent for collective action. Unfortunately, as digital social media that were more oriented toward entertainment and casual conversation became increasingly popular, they became dominated by a few overly loud voices and the sense of community and civic engagement largely evaporated.

In addition to the problem of discussions being dominated by a few "influencers" or similar disproportionately loud voices (see the digital dragons discussion in chapters 3 and 5), there are other persistent problems with using digital media for deliberation and collective action. Principal concerns among these are (1) people who interject comments that distract from prosocial, civil, and useful community conversations; (2) the rapid spreading of misinformation; and (3) a lack of participation by less wealthy and minority communities. These problems are, of course, interrelated and mutually reinforcing. Despite these problems, it may be possible to design new types of digital social media and AI to support deliberation and consensus, as laid out in a recent National Academy of Science article that I coauthored with Lily Tsai and from which the much of the following discussion is based.[2]

MODERATION (STORIES FOR ME)

The first of these problems, *disruption*, is widely dealt with by moderation. Platforms such as Reddit, where discussion forums often have strict guidelines, have human moderators that intervene to help reformulate comments so that they follow community guidelines or, failing that, they can outright reject inappropriate comments. Similarly, platforms intended for digital deliberation often include strict moderation of comments to ensure that they are civil and helpful.

Human moderation is, unfortunately, either expensive or requires unusually generous efforts by volunteers. Computers are commonly used for simple sorts of moderation, for instance, spotting banned words, but until recently more sophisticated moderation was beyond their capabilities. Today, progress in LLMs such as ChatGPT permit much more sophisticated and effective moderation and, surprisingly, *without* introducing biases, as shown in Lisa Argyle and colleagues' 2023 study.[3]

MISINFORMATION (STORIES FOR OURSELVES)

The second problem, *misinformation*, has become a serious problem in the last decade, and society at large has become very concerned about its rapid spread. It is unclear how the prevalence and effects of misinformation today compare to the situation in previous generations. It was not so long ago that disease was thought to be due to imbalances in the humors or miasma from the earth, and, as already mentioned, the fraction of US citizens who think the sun goes around the earth is greater than the fraction who believe climate change is fake.[4]

The misinformation problem has, however, changed greatly in one very significant way: False information now spreads much more quickly.[5] This rapid dissemination of misinformation likely serves to undermine the authority of statements by government experts and scientists to a greater degree than previously because the misinformation is often encountered while citizens are still considering the expert statements rather than afterward. For example, during the 2020 COVID pandemic this seems to have made successful collective action more difficult and made efforts to suppress opposing views more tempting.

The acceleration of misinformation spreading is likely due, in part, to the design of digital media platforms and business models that reward impulsive sharing. Several large-scale experiments have shown that interfaces that prompt people to reflect about accuracy before sharing can dramatically reduce the spread of misinformation.[6] A recent MIT PhD thesis by my student Ziv Epstein showed that this can be framed as a system 1 versus system 2 phenomenon as described by Daniel Kahneman.[7]

Immediate reactions to new stimuli are typically mediated by system 1 (e.g., alerting behaviors when signs of danger are detected), whereas more reflective judgments are mediated by the slower but more sophisticated cognitive mechanisms of system 2.[8]

The practical implication is that platforms intended for informing people and supporting deliberation should not offer instant reposting of information but instead promote reflection before choosing to share information. The difficulty with this solution is that it impacts the profitability of platforms based on advertising revenue, suggesting that ad-funded platforms should be restricted to entertainment and not used for large-scale news dissemination or large-scale political communications. There is a growing belief that digital platforms intended to support civic deliberation or collective action need a different business model.

INCLUSIVE DELIBERATION (STORIES FOR CHANGE)

The third problem, which is *lack of participation by marginalized communities*, is at heart the problem that the general population does not hear stories of the experiences and dreams of marginalized communities. Marginalized people know that they are not going to influence the deliberation, so why should they participate? Lack of participation stems quite logically from lack of incentives, which are a critical element of the successful functioning of any consensus network.

Consequently, we need to have a clear answer about why members of marginalized communities should incur costs in time, attention, and fees in order to help build consensus. Typical answers revolve around patriotic duty, which is a story that has grown thin. Another type of answer encourages majority communities to listen better, but there is little incentive for real engagement beyond general altruism, idealism, or a sense of duty.

For some critical communication functions such as democratic voting, nations including Australia and Brazil address this incentive problem by mandating universal participation with fines for noncompliance. These mandates are moderately successful for promoting the physical action of voting, but they do not address the sort of time-consuming, thoughtful discussion required for deliberative democracy. Consequently, even with universal voting marginalized communities still have little influence on outcomes. This is particularly frustrating because participation in debate need not be very expensive or time-consuming, and virtually everyone spends a similar amount of time and money on entertainment, gossip, and social gatherings.

INCENTIVES FOR PARTICIPATION

An intriguing idea developed in our recent design-for-democracy paper in the *Proceedings of the United States National Academy of Science* is based on the observation that the part of the population that does not participate, whether from lack of resources or because they feel they will not be listened to, is similar to the population that participates in lotteries and activities like sports betting.[9] This suggests the use of lottery-style incentives to encourage civic participation, and there is a recent study that showed promise for such incentives to expand both breadth of participation and depth of deliberation.[10] This study found that extrinsic rewards boost voting significantly and that the effects of a lottery appear to be especially strong among those of lower socioeconomic status. Importantly, the effect is probably not driven primarily by economic considerations, since the average return is quite small, but rather by the social nature of a multiperson game. I will discuss this further in the next section.

A related, better-studied intervention is the British lottery bond system, where people who save money by purchasing bonds are automatically entered into a national lottery. A large percentage of all British adults participate in this program. The evidence to date shows that lotteries can significantly improve voting participation among a population that normally has low voting participation, but more study is required to prove the causality and effectiveness of lottery incentives in a general population.

INCENTIVES FOR CONSENSUS

In both lottery incentives for voting and the British lottery bond system, the lottery creates an incentive to participate but does not create an incentive for picking a policy (from a set of suggested policies) that may eventually become law. In the context of a democratic deliberation platform like Polis (discussed in the next section), it is easy to tie the number of lottery tickets people receive to the eventual popularity of the policy they pick.

The connection between the chances of winning the lottery and the popularity of the policies supported constitutes a prediction market, where the most likely outcomes are predicted by market dynamics. As pointed out by Nobel Prize laureate Kenneth Arrow, prediction markets have long shown significant ability to predict political outcomes and can be a key part of building democratic consensus.[11]

As mentioned previously, increased participation caused by using a lottery is likely not primarily driven by a profit motive, since everyone knows the odds are stacked against them, but rather by the social interactions that are typical of such a multiperson game. Our experiments have shown that social incentives are dramatically more effective than equivalently sized direct economic incentives.[12] In China, online versions of similar social incentives, with hundreds of millions of participants, have been shown to reinforce social ties and encourage greater participation.[13]

DIGITAL CONSENSUS

In response to the decline of early, discussion-oriented social media and the rise of social media platforms designed for casual conversation and entertainment, there has been a push to develop and deploy technologies that allow people to share opinions on policy questions online and agree on recommendations. These *deliberative platforms* use tools and technologies that extend beyond conventional methods of public deliberation and promote themselves as being able to achieve deliberative goals faster, more inclusively, and at a larger scale while at the same time minimizing human bias and costs. These claims could, of course, mask a reality that looks much more like advertising or political campaigning.

We need to examine these deliberative platforms in order to see what they have to offer and whether they augment or diminish human agency. One very popular online platform that attempts to harness digital media for deliberative democracy is the Polis system, a project led by Colin Megill. It is an example of the sort of consensus network that powers science and common law. Polis is widely believed to be the most effective direct democracy social media tool, and it has been successfully used by governments on three continents.[14] Consequently, it is interesting to analyze how Polis differs from typical social media platforms and how these differences affect the human discussion.

Polis allows governments to pose policy questions to the public and then use statistical summarization to provide graphical feedback on what the population as a whole believes or desires. Coverage of Polis in the popular press claims that it is regularly effective at achieving popular consensus around contentious issues over a period of two or three weeks.

The way Polis operates is that a topic is put up for debate and then anyone who creates an (anonymous but verified) account can post comments on the topic and also upvote or downvote other people's comments. Unusually for online media, users cannot reply directly to other people's comments, making it difficult to engage in flame wars and trolling.

The upvote-downvote mechanism creates a consensus network, similar to citation networks that are the main archival mechanism for knowledge accumulation in scientific papers, patent applications, and legal decisions. In Polis, the citation network records the comments of citizens and their opinions of other people's comments. It is this record of how the collective spectrum of opinions is evolving that drives citizen interaction along with the content of the comments. If you see that certain comments are trending, or collecting lots of upvotes, then you know that the consensus is likely to move in the direction of those comments instead of others that are less popular.

A consensus network requires both connections between stories and an incentive for achieving consensus. Polis's citation network and comments provide the connections, but what about the incentive? In Polis, the framing of the systems and design of interaction encourages people to make comments that attract many upvotes, just as in scientific publications. This consensus mechanism acts to drive the evolution of comments, and so, the Polis creators explain, this is why people try to draft comments that will win votes from both sides of a divide, gradually eliminating the gaps.

Polis seems to have been most successful in Taiwan, where community self-help groups strongly incentivize participation and consensus.

Many of Taiwan's neighborhoods have community gatherings where older, more experienced people collaborate with younger, more tech-savvy people. Taiwan's community intelligence seems to include the sort of self-determination ethos that we need everywhere. In the next sections of this chapter and in the following chapter, I examine ways of using AI to expand every community's capacity for self-determination.

The Polis system uses upvotes and downvotes to generate a visualization of all the comments in the debate and uses a 1960s statistical AI method to cluster together people who have similar up- and downvotes. This sort of connection map is fairly understandable to people and frequently used in popular press, TV, and elsewhere. Even when there are hundreds or thousands of separate comments, like-minded comments cluster together in this map, showing where there are divides and where there is consensus.

The Polis user comment system enforces two important constraints that are likely critical to the success of the system. One constraint is that each individual can make only a few comments per day. Moreover, while comments are submitted anonymously, they must be made by a human whose identity and right to participate have been verified. This means that influencers, political campaigns, and companies cannot have the outsized influence that they have in regular social media, and this prevents them from dominating the deliberation.[15]

The second constraint is that people usually have to upvote and downvote other people's comments before submitting their own comment. The process of surveying people's comments for the purpose of upvoting and downvoting forces people to learn about others' opinions, and this has been shown to reliably promote wisdom-of-the-crowd effects and better decision-making.[16]

The Polis visualization of the comments, as shaped by user vote, seems to be helpful in promoting convergence of opinion, and it is much like the visualizations that have proven very effective in domains such as finance.[17] Taiwanese Minister of Information Technology Audrey Tang says, "If you show people the face of the crowd, and if you take away the reply button, then people stop wasting time on the divisive statements."[18]

Computational social science research within my research group has shown that there is reason to believe that the Polis-style, face-of-the-crowd approach will have a very significant impact on decreasing polarization. In addition to the stories-for-ourselves feedback system tested in our subversion-dilemma paper, other experiments in our research group have shown that providing users with a visualization of the range of other people's opinions and actions also improves financial decisions and interpretation of data.[19] More recently, the Polis system has inspired the creation of Community Notes on social media platforms like X, to general approval of the user community. However, this improvement does not fix all the ills of digital media.

GenAI AND DEMOCRACY

New technologies such as GenAI have already changed the nature of deliberation on policy issues on social media platforms like NextDoor. com, making discussions more civil and on point. As discussed in the previous section, features of the first generation of these platforms range from open commenting, upvoting, and simple polling to organizing assemblies and participatory budgeting. Some platforms, such as Polis, go even further, taking citizen opinions and using machine learning techniques to generate visualizations of the opinion space for users, such as areas of agreement, disagreement, and structural features intended to promote compromise or consensus.

These innovations raise important questions about how best to design these technologies so that individual rights are upheld and the discussion serves democratic objectives. Chapter 5 discussed how the ethical use of AI in social institutions should include our four principles: (1) assist but not reduce human agency; (2) treat everyone as equals; (3) protect from harm by both algorithms and bad actors; and (4) abstain from releasing us from our responsibilities or serving as our representatives.[20]

In line with these principles, the best and safest possibility for improving online deliberative democracy is by using AI to support greater user engagement and deliberation on a platform as well as to increase the inclusiveness of participation by bringing in people from all communities. At the same time, it should uphold the democratic commitments to preserving human agency, mutual respect, equality, and inclusiveness and augment active citizenship.

EXAMPLES

There are several ways to apply AI to existing deliberative platforms that are in accordance with this AI governance framework. Quite promising are AI moderation tools (e.g., AI-generated "stories for me") that remind the user to be civil and prosocial when they are contributing comments. Such AI tools are already deployed on many social network platforms, where users readily accept them, and many deployments of Polis have either human or AI comment moderation.

Going further, my former PhD student Michiel Bakker worked with researchers at DeepMind to fine-tune an LLM so that it would generate statements about policy issues that maximized the expected agreement for a group of people with diverse opinions (e.g., AI-generated "stories for ourselves"). They found that more than 65 percent of the time, study participants preferred the consensus statements generated by their model over statements written by people.[21]

While this particular AI tool may be "leading the witness" and thus reducing human agency, it suggests the potential for LLMs to help diverse groups of people find agreement. In fact, a small variation on this DeepMind AI tool could help users make more constructive and prosocial contributions to the discussion by, for example, encouraging them to consider what other people might think or how other people might view comments they contribute and whether their proposed comment might lead to consensus or prove divisive.

Another avenue for improvement is summarization and particularly visualization of community opinion (e.g., AI-generated "stories for change"). For instance, in our recent paper analyzing science, patents, and law citation networks (which are very similar to the user vote network used in Polis), we have found that we can visualize the evolution of the network in such a way that it is easy to predict convergence of the community around certain views.[22] We expect this same sort of visualization could be effective in helping citizens understand the evolution of opinion in a Polis-like platform. Such a visualization method would likely provide citizens the ability to think more clearly about the *dynamics* of political deliberation—for example, which way the discussion is trending—and then formulate responses that are more effective in achieving their aims.

In our current research, we are now beginning experimental evaluation of both the idea of AI helping people craft more effective comments and the idea of creating better visualizations of user opinion by implementing our improved understanding of citation network dynamics.[23] We expect that our investigation will provide insight into how to build effective digital democracy tools that are consistent with the principles in our framework while also clarifying the decisions we need to make about balancing these principles and protecting against the aspects of GenAI that are most dangerous for democracy.

COMMUNITY AND DEMOCRACY

Perhaps the most important problem is how to restore people's sense that they are in control of their lives and not just powerless subjects controlled by a professional management class. As I noted before, the transfer of power from communities with shared interests to professionals leaves communities (and not just physical communities) less able to innovate and means that ordinary citizens struggle to address their problems.

Communities where citizens have a concrete, visible role in deciding their future are critical. People continually repeat that voting is important, but being one of a million voters for some representative that they will never meet and who comes from a very different background is a poor substitute for a meaningful role in shaping our social institutions. Without the ability to learn, discuss, and act with people who share your situation, we quite naturally become mere spectators of the government, and our lack of engagement and focus leaves us prone to mistaken beliefs, manias, and panics of all sorts.

As a consequence, it is critical that the groups of people with whom we share common concerns—not just our physical communities but all of our communities, namely the people we work, play, and live near—have the freedom to shape their social institutions. As we have seen earlier in this book, children's development, community prosperity, and much about our culture and beliefs depend on the network of people with whom we share common concerns. When there are healthy patterns of storytelling within communities, then we can have collective decisions that are both rational and reliably better than decisions by single individuals or small groups.

The key word in these last few thoughts is "community," that is, groups of people with shared concerns who want to act collectively in order to address those concerns. Far too much of today's social and governance structure ignores communities and seeks to organize large groups of individuals for the sake of efficiency.

SUMMARY

In previous chapters I have discussed ways to use AI to support more effective and inclusive storytelling patterns and ways to help citizens see the population-wide range of attitudes in order to better understand each other and develop consensus within their communities. By establishing a community focus, we can create better bureaucracies than we have today, and that is the focus of the next chapter.

Knowing what people in your community think, and even reaching a consensus for collective action, does little without follow-up actions that fulfill the intent of the consensus. As the rate of social change moves faster and faster, our nineteenth-century bureaucracies are increasingly failing to keep up. We need a new method of collective action that is better suited to the way humans make decisions and the way human culture evolves. This chapter has outlined a promising, more inclusive method of setting policy and proposed how digital media and AI can be safely used to increase the effectiveness of policymaking without compromising human agency. Connecting policy to effective action is the focus of the next chapter.

7

BY THE PEOPLE, FOR THE PEOPLE

Creating more inclusive and engaging consensus platforms for policy decisions helps us decide which way to go but not how to get there. In modern societies we use eighteenth-century versions of legislatures to create laws and then nineteenth-century bureaucracies to implement those policies. Both legislators and bureaucracies are, of course, famously averse to change and too often self-serving. How can we use today's better understanding of people and society, together with ubiquitous digital networks and AI, to redesign our methods for decision-making and governance so that they are more respectful of individuals and communities yet at the same time more agile and effective? I will begin with a surprising example of a very hierarchical organization that used internal digital media and older AI to become much more agile, as well as a consensus organization that has quietly and very successfully created 10 percent of US law. The final part of this chapter uses these examples and the social science of Nobel Prize winner Elinor Ostrom to create a template of how to build agile, human-centered social organizations.

STORIES OF THE PAST

The top-down, command-and-control model of bureaucracy is so prevalent that it is hard to even think of another way of organizing things, and even if we did imagine something new, there would be great skepticism that it would work.

Surprisingly, some of the most critical and high-performing bureaucracies we have today, such as the US Army and commercial regulation, have reimagined traditional bureaucracy very differently. Both of these very different organizations have found ways to take advantage of instant digital information flow through email, special-purpose social media, and video conferencing on laptops and mobile phones; they show that we can rethink bureaucratic organization and that there are good ways for AI to help without endangering human agency.

For example, in 2003 the strictly hierarchical, top-down US Army—a classic bureaucratic organization—found itself confronted with a well-organized, well-funded guerila enemy in the Iraq war. The agile, distributed guerilla forces ran rings around the clunkier traditional army organization despite the army's better armament, training, and information resources, as described in General Stanley McChrystal's book *Team of Teams*.[1] The army's organization faced different problems in multiple areas, and the demands of all these problems were too complex for any one person to make all the decisions.

Therefore, the US Army was forced to adopt a far more agile organizational structure because the top-down, hierarchical management techniques were simply too slow to work in a rapidly changing environment. Led by General McChrystal, the army adopted a management style where on-the-ground teams brought in team members from logistics, intelligence, and other resource areas so they could operate as a network of teams with a shared community intelligence. Key to the success of this much more agile organization were digital networks for conversation between units and locations, previous-generation AI tools that provided contextual information for participants, and digital summaries for after-action learning. McChrystal called it the "Team of Teams" organization in his book, motivated by ideas discussed in chapters 3 and 4 of this book and my previous book *Social Physics*.[2]

An older but equally important innovation that helped make this method of organization successful was empowering every team to act as circumstances required in order to fulfill the *intent* of the commanding officer's orders rather than being constrained to follow them literally. In the US Army, a commander's intent is not just a phrase. It is a formal document shared across command levels that describes what needs to be accomplished, and this intent, not exact orders, is critical for choosing and taking action.

The effect of these changes is that leadership is distributed to lower levels of the organization and, as circumstances evolve, everyone can modify their plans so that they satisfy the commander's intent. By breaking up administrative units and replacing them with distributed leadership and an agile team-of-teams structure that evolves according to need, this formerly rigid bureaucracy was transformed into a hybrid organization. It retained a hierarchical command structure to bear responsibility for outcomes but dramatically broadened the set of people involved in planning and carrying out each action on an as-needed basis. It became an organization where every stakeholder team could contribute toward shaping the final plan of action and was included in after-operations reviews that helped evolve the planning and decision structure. The resulting structure is rather like the famous Toyota quality circles, where regular bottom-up feedback helps shape decisions, and it is similar to the stories-for-ourselves and stories-for-change ideas introduced earlier.

The experience of the US Army suggests several attributes that are essential for an agile, effective organization. Among these attributes are that (1) those responsible for solving the problem make up the strategies for tackling the problem; (2) all the stakeholders must be involved; (3) bottom-up feedback and discussion drive team leaders' decisions; and (4) it is the intended goals, and not the exact rules or orders, that matter.

It is useful to compare this approach to the fixed hierarchies and rule-based behavior of standard bureaucracies. Imagine that regulatory procedures were regularly evaluated by social outcomes and updated, and that employees who saw standard approaches failing were (within bounds) free to try new approaches in order to meet the intent of the law or regulation. Imagine if employees who discovered better approaches were personally rewarded and their innovations publicized so that others could try them elsewhere.

We have all heard stories of this sort of organizational innovation, and many of our bureaucratic best practices evolved in this way. But usually it takes great courage to step outside of bureaucracy's standard operating procedure. Imagine if this sort of innovation were systematically supported—if the US Army can do it, then we can do it elsewhere as well.

CONSENSUS NETWORKS FOR PUBLIC ADMINISTRATION

The team-of-teams approach shows that digital networks for just-in-time discussion and dissemination of crucial information, together with

AI for context awareness and summarization, can help even very rigid bureaucracies become agile. Maybe elephants really can learn to dance. The team-of-teams approach is also suitable for other organizations that have great urgency to act and a dangerous environment, such as a startup company. Andrew McAfee, for instance, argues that this general type of organization is why Silicon Valley startups are so successful.[3]

Unfortunately, the time pressure under which such organizations operate limits inclusivity and makes complex innovation very difficult. In the previous chapter I described how consensus networks can allow much larger numbers of people to participate and can be better at finding compromise. As a consequence, consensus networks may be better suited for civilian organizations. To answer the question about how this might work in practice, let us examine the 150-year-old consensus network that manages the US Uniform Commercial Code (UCC; introduced in chapter 4).

The US Uniform Law Commission, which supports the UCC, is a not-for-profit, volunteer organization that uses a consensus network of lawyers who examine which laws should be modified in order to make interstate commerce more seamless.[4] Today this debate benefits from digital networks for sharing information and discussing issues, along with older-style AI for modeling market effects and financial flows. It combines a debate about what laws to adopt with the very strong incentive of enabling orderly cross-border trade, and this incentive quite reliably induces legislators, bureaucracies, and private actors to conform to the consensus.

It is important to remind readers that the commission does not pass laws, but it does recommend laws and regulations to each of the US states. There is a strong incentive for states to enact these suggestions in order to make trade with other states as smooth as possible.

The UCC benefits from an active, highly incentivized consensus network that includes all economic actors, not only lawyers, and they are all actively engaged in deliberation and discussion. This is similar to the consensus networks seen in science, medicine, patents, and courts: They each depend on strong personal incentives for participation, deliberation, and consensus.

What distinguishes this approach to ensuring compatibility and coordination between state laws is not only these strong incentives but also that (1) there are detailed statistics and older-style AI predictions about trade at every level of government and in every part of commerce; (2) everyone is very aligned in their desire for greater prosperity; and (3) as a consequence, everyone pays close attention to trade numbers and actively advocates for changes that will benefit themselves or their community. Each of these three characteristics seems to be essential for the rather amazing track record that this approach to commercial regulation has achieved.

How could we implement this type of consensus process elsewhere in society? Comparison to public services where governance is top-down or examples where a public consensus process already exists suggests that in top-down situations there are three major missing pieces. First of all, there is often a lack of transparency, with few properly scoped, timely, and trustworthy data. For example, domains such as policing, education, and public health could all benefit from more transparent and trustworthy performance data. While some data are available in these areas, they often suffer from being too infrequent, aggregated, and indirect. Providing such data is the stories-for-ourselves and stories-for-me idea discussed throughout this book.

Second, for many public services, there is currently nothing like a Polis-style digital deliberation platform, and even more importantly, there is no strong, individually relevant incentive mechanism. Usually the incentives are to "be a good citizen" or "support your neighbor," which are not comparable to incentives like "be able to care for your children."

And third, the forces of centralization have mis-scoped the governance so that questions that concern only a few members of one community are decided by voters, bureaucracies, laws, and legislators that administer much larger groups of people. People are forced to manage their commons according to the notions of distant and unrelated people.

GOVERNMENT IS FOR REGULATING THE COMMONS

The research of Nobel Prize winner Elinor Ostrom illuminates how best to structure governance problems of all sorts. Her research characterizes the commonalities in the approaches that different people and different communities all around the world have developed to successfully manage common resources.[5] What is perhaps most surprising about her studies is the similarity in how commons have been managed, independent of culture, resources, education, and other variables. These same principles are, unsurprisingly, found in the team-of-teams and consensus network approaches to management.

We can group Ostrom's findings into three principles that characterize successful management of common resources, and which let us connect her work to the terminology and organization of this book:

1. *First principle: Governance by the governed; clearly defined boundaries; rules apply within boundaries but not elsewhere; nested governance for nested commons*

    Communities need clear membership criteria and need to be able to organize themselves in order to adapt to their unique conditions. There is the need for nested governance: Parking might, for instance, be governed by each city precinct but the overall functionality of the road system needs to involve the entire city, while safety policy for vehicle manufacturers should include the whole nation. However, rather than placing central bureaucracy in charge, consensus mechanisms could be used, similar to how the Uniform Commercial Code is continually updated.

2. *Second principle: Reliable monitoring; graduated sanctions for violations of rules and associated conflict-resolution mechanisms*

    There can be no rational planning without evidence, and collective action requires collective solidarity, which means we need individual compliance. The Bronze rule—to treat others like you would want to be treated, but not to be infinitely forgiving—is known to provide the best incentive for solidarity and cooperation. There needs to be a strong, transparent, and yet forgiving enforcement mechanism.

3. *Third principle: Congruence between citizen contributions, benefits, and local conditions*

    Democratic governance should reflect deliberation by the entire citizenship of the commons. Rules and benefits should be as evidence based as possible, and the intended benefits and costs of each policy decision should be explicit and regularly reviewed, like in the team-of-teams organization or the quality circles organization made popular by Toyota.[6]

The rest of this section explores these three principles in greater depth.

FIRST OSTROM PRINCIPLE: SOCIAL INSTITUTIONS ARE FOR REGULATING THE COMMONS

Perhaps the most important change is to accept that government exists for the management of the *commons* and not to force people to live in particular ways. How can we structure this sort of government of the commons?

Ostrom's work suggests that shared resources—called a "commons" after the commonly owned fields used for cattle and sheep grazing since the Middle Ages—need to be governed by the people who are substantial participants in the commons. Governance of these commons should be by the communities themselves. Communities are defined by *common concerns*, not just physical proximity, and each commons has an associated community of members and an area of common concern. Research has shown that debates are more effective when conducted among people who have common concerns and incentives to act collectively.

Just as each individual is a member of many communities, they are also participants in many commons, that is, in many groups of people with shared concerns and resources. Furthermore, each commons must be cooperatively managed in order to achieve life, liberty, and the pursuit of happiness. In other words, our social institutions should not be dictating the behavior of people outside the specific topics of common concern or outside the community associated with that commons. That, of course, requires consensus networks like the one that guides the evolution of the UCC so that communities do not impinge on one another and are held accountable to their citizens.

SECOND OSTROM PRINCIPLE: DATA FOR TRANSPARENCY, ACCOUNTABILITY, AND GUARDRAILS

Good decision-making requires having knowledge of the current situation, what other communities have done in similar situations, and how their actions succeeded or failed to address their problems.

The invention of the census as a tool of government and business in the early nineteenth century dramatically improved the reliability of policy and planning. This is the stories-for-ourselves idea. Our census today counts physical and economic characteristics, but it does not count the connections between communities, workplaces, or other resources. We need enhanced census data that also provide evidence about the social situation and how each community is embedded within society—at a minimum, where they work, shop, and play.

As part of the United Nations Secretary General's Data Revolutionaries team, I collaborated with a group that was charged with envisioning how data and AI were going to be used for planning and monitoring progress on the Sustainable Development Goals (SDGs).[7] Inspired in part by a series of nationwide "Living Lab" experiments that my collaborators and I conducted in Senegal, Côte d'Ivoire, Italy, and the United Kingdom, the Data Revolutionaries proposed constructing "enhanced census" metrics for monitoring progress toward each of the United Nations' 17 SDGs (e.g., poverty reduction, environmental sustainability, reduction in inequality, etc.) within each country.

Our UN team recognized that certain enhanced census data can provide the scientific determination of what policies are likely to be successful.[8] As a consequence, the idea of privacy-safe, enhanced census data is the foundation of measuring progress toward the 2015 SDGs, and these measures are already helping decision-makers in many low- and mid-income countries tackle societal problems such as poverty, inequality, and sustainability.

An example of using these sorts of data is the Nobel Prize–winning work of MIT researchers Esther Duflo and Abhijit Banerjee.[9] They used these richer census measures to examine many very similar villages, and they encouraged half of the villages to institute a new social policy. Later they could measure the effect of the policy by comparing villages that experimented with the new policy versus villages without the new policy. This allowed the researchers to find policies that reliably promoted economic development in low-income countries.

Governments are sometimes embarrassed by such data and stories because they can highlight policy failures, and so access is often restricted to government bureaucracies. The best examples today of public stories-for-ourselves facilities are Harvard Growth Lab's Atlas of Economic Complexity and the surprisingly accurate World Factbook published by the US Central Intelligence Agency in order to help fight disinformation that would-be dictators and revolutionaries sometimes spread about trade, health, and other issues.[10]

Consensus networks like those found in the fields of science and medicine have worked reliably for centuries, and fully digital consensus platforms like Polis have a good track record for helping communities productively debate what actions to take. Some nations do the same with rich census statistics about communities in order to discover improved policies and regulations. Instead of requiring the best scientists and years of effort by a sizable team, this sort of evidence mining can be done locally by the communities themselves.

Today, new stories-for-ourselves AI systems are being commercially deployed in business by Amazon, Salesforce, Microsoft, and others. This prompts the question, Why can't citizens everywhere do the same for their communities? Companies are willing and able to provide stories-for-ourselves platforms to government. Now citizens need to demand that governments populate these platforms with the data the government currently has so that citizens can hold government accountable for the outcomes of their policies and so that citizens can intelligently debate what new policies might be better.

THIRD OSTROM PRINCIPLE: RESOURCES AND INCENTIVES FOR MANAGEMENT OF THE COMMONS

A critical question that is inevitably raised whenever anyone proposes that communities control their social institutions is where the financial resources come from. Individuals who live in underserved communities do not generally have much money and so cannot be expected to pay for the infrastructure they might need. It is therefore important to note that we already spend a lot of money on these communities; the money generally does not go to the community itself, however, but rather to professional managers who typically live in other, more wealthy communities.

In the United States, there is about one social services worker for every 25 households living below the poverty line. These workers control somewhere between $11,000 and $45,000 of annual services per household.[11] Although the true cost is hotly debated, the average social services worker may cost the government about $130,000 per year, including salary and overhead. Unfortunately very few of these workers live in the neighborhoods they serve, so their salaries and benefits flow to more wealthy neighborhoods, and their understanding of life in the communities they serve is necessarily limited. If we gave neighborhood communities more control over *existing* city, state, and federal community spending, allowing them to tailor local policing, schools, public health, and social support services to better suit their community's conditions, we could rekindle democratic participation and cause a sea change in trust in government and our social institutions.

We are so used to top-down bureaucracies that local control sounds like a recipe for anarchy and disaster. But this is exactly the way that the United States was governed at its founding. Towns and states did things their own way, and this worked because travel was difficult and there was little interaction. Every town, every state, was its own little country. As the population grew, roads were developed, canals were dug, and railways were built, which meant that coordination became important. Thus, institutions like the Uniform Law Commission were created to harmonize trade, ownership rights, and other areas of law and regulation that were part of a commons between states or between towns.

It was only after the superhighways were finished and digital communications became common that cost pressures caused centralization to take off. It was cheaper and easier to impose uniform solutions than to reach a compromise that benefited everyone. The availability of 1960s and 1980s AI made centralization easy to accomplish. Unfortunately, the consequence was that regulation became one-size-fits-none, so that atypical communities, such as minority or low-income communities, were disadvantaged.

Today, technological progress has forged *distributed* digital systems—where control spreads among all the stakeholders—that are even cheaper than central administration and also more resistant to failures and attacks.[12] This is why large telephone companies do not control telephone traffic centrally and why the internet architecture has been so successful. Today, even older, simpler, and more transparent AI allows us to coordinate local policies quickly and at low cost, and GenAI methods can suggest ways to coordinate that can dramatically accelerate consensus among stakeholders (see discussion at the end of chapter 6, for instance).[13]

THE PATH TO GOVERNMENT BY THE PEOPLE, FOR THE PEOPLE

Our current institutions fail to adhere to any of these three Ostrom principles. Perhaps the major source of this failure comes from violations of the first principle, governance by the governed and clear boundaries. Two centuries ago, it was hard for one community to interfere with, or even be aware of, the affairs of a different community. In the US, governance was by the governed, and physical distance set most of the boundaries. Today, cars, trains, airplanes, and digital communications ensure that almost no community is really separated from the others.

GOVERNANCE BY THE WRONG PEOPLE

With the advent of digital technologies, it became easy to use centralized systems to manage community-specific problems if the problems were at least superficially similar. Centralization, however, brought unintended consequences. For example, banking and medical practice used to be mostly governed locally but are now typically centralized across the entire country, which disadvantages people of color, women, and minorities.

Similarly, instead of having local services managed at the neighborhood level, policies about services such as fees charged, licensing, and so forth are too often set at the city or even state level. The tendency to centralize government sometimes overrides local control even when it results in worse outcomes. For instance, in Britain, giving local councils the power to manage their neighborhood services was quite successful, but the councils lacked the political clout to survive budget cuts. Another example is in Chicago Public Schools. When schools in Chicago were given the freedom to act independently, educational quality improved dramatically. Sadly, the schools were recentralized as Chicago Mayor Richard M. Daley built his patronage network.[14]

BLURRY BOUNDARIES

Following the rule that governance should be by the governed requires us to pay much more attention to the second part of the first principle, which is to have clear boundaries about what communities of common interest exist and who belongs to those communities. But, of course, different communities will have different rules and norms, so how can we reconcile these differences? Typically, people resort to top-down rulemaking, which violates the first principle. A better way is through the sort of consensus network that drives the UCC, or perhaps the team-of-teams approach for urgent problems.

The failure to have clear boundaries makes it easy to argue for governance that is more centralized. The prevalence of one-size-fits-none policies, such as those that plague the European Union and the Heartland-versus-Coast political battles seen in the United States, is a critical test of whether these boundaries are set correctly. Any uniform rule is likely to be good for the "average" community but inappropriate for communities that are marginalized, minority, or just different. Centralization not only leaves citizens frustrated, it also destroys trust in government. Governance should be by the governed.

RELIABLE MONITORING AND DISPUTE RESOLUTION

To be successful, local governance requires monitoring of communities to make sure they comply with guardrails and to give feedback to the community about the effectiveness of their policies. With modern digital infrastructure, we no longer need centralization to enforce better behavior and can hold communities responsible to their members by regularly publishing census-like statistics to evaluate local policies.

By having regular information about government costs and policy outcomes, we can much more easily manage problems like fraud, favoritism, bias, and so on than was possible even a decade ago. This type of auditing is a very promising area for GenAI, and already there are examples of using GenAI to detect fraud that have been extremely successful.

Importantly, such local statistics can make it easier for local groups to jointly resist budget cuts and recentralization. In fact, digital accountability is a key point of the UN SDGs, and the open data movement in many countries is also a product of this thinking. A strong example of census-like data being used toward digital accountability is found in the United Kingdom's Office for National Statistics, as shown at https://www.ons.gov.uk/help/localstatistics, which was created to help management of the local councils. These local statistics, provided by the central government, help citizens keep local government accountable.

However, data on a community's health are useless unless the community understands what the data mean and what policy options are likely to improve any problems. Citizens need shared knowledge about what other communities have done to address their problems and how their actions worked or failed. Public studies of what works and what does not, along with citizen education in understanding and using such data, can allow communities to learn from each other and, over time, shape social institutions that work better for themselves.

AI tools such as the "stories for ourselves" mentioned earlier, which allow individuals to better understand their communities and explore other communities, are critical. A telling example is the polarization story in chapter 4, where we found that we could very substantially reduce political polarization in the United States by using a simple version of the stories-for-ourselves tool to provide information about what the "other guys" actually think rather than forcing citizens to rely on declarations by ambitious politicians and journalists whose salaries depend on the number of views they get.[15]

TRUST AND COLLECTIVE ACTION

Today fewer than 20 percent of people in the United States say that they trust the government to do the right thing most of the time, whereas 80 percent trusted the government in 1960.[16] Much of this collapse in trust may be due to central control and the resulting disenfranchisement of communities. Centralization enabled services to become cheaper and more uniform, but communities lost their local institutions and the skills, engagement, and local knowledge that go with them. As a result, communities also lost control over their money, their health, and the ability to govern themselves. By the year 2000, the deployment of centralized data and early AI systems had disenfranchised communities to such an extent that Robert Putnam's book *Bowling Alone* described the change as the collapse of community social structure.

People wonder why there is so little trust in today's institutions and why people do not vote or participate. I think that the answer is obvious:

centralization means that individuals and their communities are disenfranchised, governed from afar by people with concerns that are quite different from their own. It is basic logic that if the actions of a person or institution do not fit your understanding of what would be beneficial, then it is probably wise not to trust them. Moreover, if you are not part of the ruling group, then it is difficult to know their thoughts and plans and why they make choices that hurt you and your community. Without intimate familiarity, it is natural, and logical, to be suspicious of motives and true intentions.

WHAT COULD REAL COMMUNITY GOVERNANCE LOOK LIKE?

While it might seem overly romanticized, the 1946 Christmas film *It's a Wonderful Life* illustrated the value of community members working together to invest in their communities and build better lives. It also mirrored the 1950s political platform of "community capitalism" that guided America's recovery from the debt load and social dislocations of the Great Depression and World War II.

We should not take examples like this as simply nostalgia for older ways of behaving but rather as a first draft that captures an essential truth about human nature and cultural evolution. At the center of this vision are community members investing their time and effort to build the future they want for both their neighbors and their children—very different from the anonymous, income-maximizing "big capital" investment we see today, with huge companies dominating our lives. It really does take a village to help people thrive, and our challenge today is to harness digital technology to update this truth to suit our turbulent, uncertain times.

Largely unappreciated by current social institutions, this vision of community self-determination leverages the truth that human collective action depends on story sharing, trust, and social capital within communities. In the 1950s and 1960s, community-based collective action in the United States had a large, positive impact on the country. For instance, 56 percent of the US electricity grid was built by community cooperatives during this period. Similarly, financial stability came to many communities by way of the credit unions and cooperatives established during that period. Many of the things we assume were done by the government turn out to be due to community action.

Perhaps even more importantly, these efforts helped build the social capital and community autonomy that gave support to the civil rights movement and related social reforms of 1960s America. Civic advocacy societies, including activist churches and community co-ops, arose in communities across the United States, advocating not only for citizen and worker rights but also for self-determination. There was a sense that communities could take hold of their fate and create environments that would help them thrive.

COMMUNITY DATA TRUSTS FOR COMMUNITY EMPOWERMENT

How can we revive the ability for communities to take action to improve their situation? A critical part of self-determination is control of the resources needed to support collective action. In the late 1800s and early 1900s, labor unions were formed, with many being only local at first. In addition, the United States saw the growth of agricultural co-ops that provided loans and other farming services.

Today, data are a primary means of production, and they offer a way to restore local trust and agency. Data trusts could help community members manage their data and what they expose to companies—since companies would no longer be able to access your data directly.[17] Many countries are pursuing this path in legislation, and it was a major theme at the 2023 G20 meeting in India.[18]

In a world where each person's data are managed by their community-owned data trust, when a person wants health care services or to make a purchase, they do not share their data with the hospital or company. Instead, their community data trust shares—and also audits—the specific data required under legal terms established by the community trust. This makes control of data easy for citizens; they just join a community trust whose policies they like.

This idea of having a local institution help people keep track of data is very much what we do today with money and banks. Credit cards, checks, and similar instruments give instructions to your bank to send money to merchants for specific goods and services. Banks do not own your money. They manage it for you—and so would data trusts. Part of the interest in the idea of community data trusts is that it would take relatively little effort to extend the existing payment infrastructure that allows us to control and audit our money to one where data trusts could provide similar control and auditing for data sharing.

This type of evolution of personal ownership rights over data was first demonstrated at scale in Estonia, which back in the mid-1990s converted its government data systems to be more accountable to citizens. More recently iSpirit, an open-source, not-for-profit group in India, has created a data commons called the "India Stack," which is like a version of the web that supports secure transactions. This system is now used by more than a billion people, even by the lowest-income people, to trade, borrow, and have legal representation.[19] This Indian invention has now spread to 26 other countries under the name the "Citizen Stack" and has hundreds of millions of users around the Indo-Pacific region in addition to India's billion users.[20]

For people who worry about the role of government in systems like the India Stack, there are green shoots appearing in the United States as well. As mentioned earlier my research group has worked with Consumer Union (publisher of Consumer Reports) to deploy a quite successful consumer app called Permission Slip, which helps people manage and control their personal data.

Just as we invented credit unions to help community members manage their money, we can have data trusts to help citizens manage their data, licensing them for use only when it is in the interest of the community members and when there are legal guarantees that sharing will not leak the data elsewhere. In fact, many if not most credit unions are already legally chartered to *be* data trusts if we decide that is what we want; new laws are not required.

Data trusts can also help future-proof us. As AI and data analytics tools grow more sophisticated, the primary limit on the power of these tools is the availability of data. Those firms that control the most data may become "data dragons" and have the ability to exert outsized influence on citizens. By adopting solutions as Estonia or India have, communities can successfully compete against big corporations and big government. If individuals and communities have control of the data that are used to manage services and investments in their community, they can leverage their own data rather than simply giving them away as we do today.

SUMMARY

To reform our governments and social institutions so that they follow the Ostrom principles and avoid reliance on a small, professional class of administrators to manage society, we need different ways of organizing ourselves and different ways of sharing our stories. Digital technologies such as AI hold great promise but to date have come with unintended, negative consequences such as the spread of misinformation, the creation of echo chambers, and increased centralization and polarization.

To avoid these problems, we need to design digital media and new AI technologies to suit humans and the way *people* think. We are not independent, rational actors; rather we are members of many different types of communities, each defined by common interests and concerns. Our community intelligence, built from the stories we tell each other, guides most of our behavior and is a critical contributor to robust and adaptive decision-making. We need to design our digital systems to recognize and leverage these basic facts of human nature.

In this chapter I have focused on two examples. First, I described the team-of-teams organization as a "halfway" step toward the sort of bureaucracies we want and a proof-of-principle that more agile bureaucracies are possible even for the most difficult, time-critical social problems. The second example was the Uniform Law Commission, which shows that consensus organizations can work quite well over the long term. The performance of both of these organizations has been successfully enhanced by digital communications and (older types) of AI functioning in the human-centric manner suggested in the first half of this book.

Finally, I described the lessons from these examples in terms of the Ostrom principles, which give us a concrete recipe for designing the sort of social institutions that best suit humans and the types of digital media and AI that fit within those principles. The detailed process of building such new institutions, or modifying existing institutions, is not the task of this book. Such reinvention needs to be done inclusively, by both the readers of this book and the rest of the citizenry, perhaps using the methods outlined in the previous chapter.

8

GETTING THERE: REGULATION AND GLOBAL COOPERATION

Our transformation from just another ape species to a world explorer may well have begun through our habits of sharing stories around a campfire in a way that encouraged greater exploration. The creation of the first civilizations may have depended on harnessing the greater opportunities created by sharing stories between diverse groups of people. And the explosion of innovation called the Enlightenment most certainly depended on the development of consensus networks that allow people to assess relationships between stories and to determine which are more likely to be useful.

As a species, we prevailed in the past mainly because small groups of humans were able to act collectively and find new ways of living. Today we need innovation and coordinated action at a greater scale than ever before if we are to surmount the current dangers of climate change, health crises, pollution, and more. What can we possibly do that will work?

I think that our real problem in dealing with issues such as climate change or health crises is our inability to achieve and maintain the consensus needed to act decisively. In other words, the solution to our problems may be the same as it was for these previous cultural revolutions: invent better ways to discuss, decide, and act. AI systems that are cooperatively synergistic may help us build the human-driven deliberation and collective action platforms we need to solve our pressing global challenges.

In this book I have shown many examples where both older AI and newer GenAI supercharge our ability to innovate and act collectively, and I have pointed out that it is usually centralizing forces that hinder human agency and diminish our ability to innovate, explore, and act collectively. We are continually tempted to make rules about how other people should behave, ignoring that this disenfranchises many and undermines the shared wisdom that is the real strength of our communities. The failure of current systems to address global problems forces us to think seriously about how we can use the power of AI, the internet, and other technologies to create a community intelligence and consensus process that spans all of humanity and enables productive collective action.

A critical and underappreciated requirement for worldwide collective action is that there needs to be sufficient operational uniformity among different nations so that companies do not seek out the weakest regulatory regime. There should also be fairly simple, inexpensive interoperability across nations, similar to the interoperability we see in trade and finance, in order to avoid disadvantaging individual citizens, smaller companies, and developing nations.

BEGIN WHERE WE STAND: INTERNATIONAL CONSENSUS ORGANIZATIONS

An almost universal problem with our current thinking about AI is that it is too parochial. Sometimes discussions raise the specter of competition with China or consider regulatory cooperation with the European Union, but rarely in my experience do they consider the broader range of players and technology possibilities. As someone who is intimately familiar with India, Singapore, Abu Dhabi, and others, I can tell you this is a serious mistake.

In a five- to ten-year time frame, many players will have the competitive technical capability needed to bring AI to transform their business, trade, health, and military capacities. Furthermore, constraints on computing hardware availability and energy use are already evaporating as new software and hardware architectures are developed, and problems of data availability will produce a functioning data market for general data and proprietary solutions for specific business and government processes. The spread and capabilities of the most important AI technologies will be significantly shaped by forces and opportunities *outside* the United States, China, and the European Union.

Two years ago, I led a discussion on AI and leadership at the Club de Madrid, whose members are the former presidents and prime ministers of all the world's democratic nations, in a meeting supported by BertelsmannStiftung and Boston Global Forum that included leading AI regulators. A sobering aspect of this discussion was that few if any of the regulators participating seemed willing to consider anything other than limiting AI development through rigid, top-down regulation focused on today's hot-button topics. The idea of AI as an opportunity to be nurtured and cultivated seemed alien to them.

The most striking example of the impulse for top-down regulation was the split between the senior EU regulators and the former national leaders. The regulators insisted on new laws and bureaucracies to control AI. That is, they wanted ex-ante regulation (i.e., regulation before deployment) tailored for each different type of AI. The national leaders, in contrast, liked the idea of auditing AI behavior and letting liability and civil law decisions shape the use of AI because this approach can be quickly implemented in a sensible, efficient manner. The approach of open audit trails enables both rapid detection of harm and rapid regulatory enforcement. In addition, because it naturally adapts to encompass further innovation, it would likely be able to deal with new types of AI and changing circumstances.

Importantly, the idea of requiring open, continuous audit trails is also critical for addressing existential risks. Most of the negative effects of digital social media were unexpected and thus invisible to regulators. It is only by continuously monitoring the effects of a technology that you can hope to limit its misuse or unexpected negative effects. In both my view and the view of EU leaders, the audit trail and liability approach is much more likely to achieve a desirable result. Amusingly, the regulators described this ex-post (after the fact) approach as being "too Anglo-Saxon" for the European Union and insisted on centralized control.

From this discussion it became obvious to me that the best place to start building a worldwide framework for the use of AI is by harnessing the international organizations that are already built on consensus networks and which currently manage much of our global commons. Examples of these *consensus organizations* are global standards bodies such as the Internet Experts Task Force (IETF), which determines how the global internet functions; the Financial Action Task Force (FATF), which establishes best practices to minimize fraud and criminal activity around the world; and the International Health Regulator (IHR), part of the World Health Organization, which helps nations coordinate public health action.

Problems of communication, commerce, and health spread through the networks of interaction that support our societies. These problems can affect everyone. However, each nation has special concerns that must be taken into account in order to have consensus and effective collective action. Consensus organizations usually have little actual power to enforce behavior. Instead, coordination must be driven by the self-interest of each nation, company, and individual. They need to cooperate for their own selfish good.

Despite the lack of enforcement power, these international consensus organizations usually work surprisingly well, especially as compared to, for instance, the United Nations or the World Bank, which are dominated by only a few nations.[1] Importantly, in the last few decades we have seen that the effectiveness of consensus organizations can be dramatically improved by use of (older) AI and the sort of privacy-preserving cryptography tools found at http://transformers.mit.edu.

This improvement is driven by the fact that all of these consensus organizations require the use of specific data to learn what works, coordinate actions, audit outcomes, and make decisions. It is critical that the privacy and quality of these operational data be maintained. Recent improvements to these international consensus organizations include technologies such as AI for early warning signals, distributed ledgers for fraud resistance, cryptography for controlled privacy, and secure digital identity. These new digital technologies improve the consensus process by enabling them to have continuous, transparent audit trails for oversight and coordination, together with continuous measurement of outcomes for policymaking, and accountability through open publishing of outcomes.

Instead of imposing new top-down rules, further improvement in the performance of these consensus organizations seems the best way to address the world's problems. This approach avoids the rigidity and one-size-fits-none policymaking problems that plague top-down, centralized approaches. These technological improvements happen organically, of course, but as a piecemeal patchwork without the vision of the larger picture being discussed here. Digital technology, however, reaches everywhere. Piecemeal solutions will not work.

THE INTERNET IS EVOLVING

Another nearly universal problem with discussions about the use of AI is that we are in the middle of a digital earthquake, such that today's exciting solutions quickly become tomorrow's obsolete ideas. There is a tsunami of new technology coming, and today's social disruptions are the first symptoms of much bigger changes to come. The reason is that the basic nature of the internet is being transformed, evolving from a loosely structured communications medium to a trusted execution medium. Digital identity, cryptography, AI, and other technologies have the potential to finally allow both companies and citizens to safely and securely do business with each other—to let each party know who they are dealing with, confirm that the interaction is not fraudulent, and guarantee the outcomes. But we need to address some key challenges to allow these technologies to best serve humanity.

The current changes we are seeing are a logical extension of the technology evolution we have been witnessing for the past 70 years, certainly since the first computers were invented and the early days of the ARPANET (US Advanced Research Projects Agency Network), the predecessor of today's internet. It is worthwhile to understand the history of the ARPANET, whose original intent was to keep military communications safe in case of a nuclear attack. The system was later extended to keep municipalities and universities connected and to protect other important information. But because all the users of these early systems were either government or university personnel, the early internet did not need to provide the sort of security and auditability required by an open, global internet, and so the current internet has not fully developed the trusted systems we need in order to run our society.

AI and other distributed digital security technologies, like distributed ledgers and zero-knowledge proofs, are part of a set of evolving global technoeconomic structures that are better suited for a connected world. We are entering an era where we cannot afford to have our digital systems fail, and so we must guarantee that data and analysis systems are secure and functioning properly. Imagine being able to monitor transactions from anywhere on the planet and be confident that they are secure, that your data are not stolen, and that money and goods always get to where they are supposed to go quickly and safely.

KEY INTERNATIONAL CHALLENGES

To have a healthy ecosystem that can leverage technologies like AI safely and successfully with each country, we must have guardrails internationally. What sorts of regulatory topics are missing from discussions within our current international systems? I think there are three main areas where international agreement and transnational initiatives could make an important difference to the smooth functioning of consensus organizations: (1) outcomes data for transparency, forecasting, and accountability; (2) auditing of AI and digital transactions for standards enforcement; and (3) governance to set rules for digital platforms.

The shared need of all nations to work across national boundaries to support trade, investment, health, and security can be the force that guides the evolution of these three areas, although complete uniformity is impossible due to differing norms and local conditions. Instead, discussions should focus on establishing norms of interaction, auditing, accountability, and governance between communities that are acceptable to all, much as payments and trade norms are today, largely due to their respective consensus organizations. It is important to note that these requirements echo the Ostrom principles discussed in the previous chapter.

REQUIREMENT 1: OUTCOMES DATA FOR TRANSPARENCY, FORECASTING, AND ACCOUNTABILITY

Both the financial crash of 2008 and the recent pandemic have laid bare the inadequacy of current systems, both in terms of their inability to forecast and manage crises and in terms of their systemic exclusion or bias against many parts of society. To build inclusive, innovative, and equitable global systems, there needs to be access to robust, timely, and comprehensive data that are like current census and economic data but enriched to include many aspects of social health (e.g., the set of social conditions that enable thriving communities).

As my research partners and I emphasized in the 2022 and 2024 G20 meetings, open access to these sorts of data will allow stakeholders to anticipate sources of local and global risks more quickly and with greater certainty, to help with financial crashes, climate change, pandemics, and other sorts of social distress. The data resources outlined by the United

Nations' SDGs, for instance, envision having trustworthy, open, and accountable access to real-time, comprehensive, and granular data that allow understanding of the situation of individual communities without threatening the privacy of individuals.

Such data can enable governments and policymakers to ensure that policies perform as intended and without negative side effects. For example, the Organization for Economic Cooperation (OECD) dialogue on data taxes could be framed using metrics created to measure progress toward the SDGs. This could potentially allow tax systems to assess tax not only on income but on environmental impact, inequality impact, public health measures, and so on. It is for this reason that the OECD, WEF, United Nations, and others are developing comprehensive data standards that will apply not only to economics but also to sustainability and governance.

REQUIREMENT 2: SECURITY FOR AI SYSTEMS AND DIGITAL TRANSACTIONS

Foundational to the digital transformation of nations will be the need for strengthened multilateral cooperation to ensure the privacy of citizens and the security of both public and private data systems (e.g., government systems, financial systems, health systems, etc.). A strengthened commitment to multilateral cybersecurity is increasingly urgent for many nations.

As AI and Internet-of-Things technologies are more widely deployed in the coming years, many nations will face increasingly disruptive cyberattacks. Current estimates project that the frequency of such attacks could be an order of magnitude greater than today's and would threaten basic government, health, food, power, and financial systems. Similarly, the impending deployment of national digital currencies may pose an even greater danger. Not only could hacks of a national digital currency cause immense real-world damage, but such systems can potentially allow the tracking of every purchase for every person. Such individual-level financial tracking poses privacy risks that dwarf current concerns.

Coordinated multinational and national systems that allow unified and agile responses are required. The need for technologies such as secure, privacy-preserving digital ID, accurate records of cross-border trade, and real-time sharing of health data is becoming urgent. There are, of course, many relevant initiatives underway, but there is no overarching vision—so gaps and contradictions abound. The technology to build effective systems exists, and the industry is willing to lead the way in deployment. Now governments need to enable effective, coordinated detection of attacks, fraud, and rules for proportional response.

REQUIREMENT 3: INTEROPERABLE GOVERNANCE FOR DIGITAL PLATFORMS

Modernizing and digitizing governance of national, international, and commercial interactions to become more efficient, transparent, and inclusive is a key global priority. Dozens of efforts are already underway but, again, current efforts are mostly piecemeal and incremental.

Governance of digital platforms has become unexpectedly urgent with the deployment of nationally backed digital systems that support not only financial transactions but also trade and logistics, authentication, fraud detection, and analytics. China, for instance, is moving existing Silk Road investments onto Chinese digital systems that are dramatically more agile and cheaper than Western systems. Singapore has developed a similar digital trade and logistics infrastructure for investments within its Temasek sovereign wealth fund, and Switzerland is experimenting with the Swiss Trust Chain. Finally, most major economies have either deployed or are seriously considering deployment of national digital currencies.

New digital platforms using AI, distributed ledgers, zero-knowledge proofs, and novel cryptographic methods are poised to integrate the majority of the world's trade into efficient, unified frameworks that seamlessly interoperate across sovereign and institutional borders. However, the standards for accountability, inclusiveness, and governance are defined quite differently in different countries. It is imperative that nations engage in standards harmonization for these digital systems in the same way they have historically reached consensus around payments, trade, and public health.

COOPERATIVE REGULATION OF AI

To understand how best to shape law to achieve cooperative, interoperable international regulation, members of my research group (and especially JD-PhD student Robert Mahari) and I have engaged with the EU AI Act authors, the authors of the Biden Executive Order on AI, and civil authorities in several Indo-Pacific countries. We noted that most of the leading AI countries have a well-developed and generally similar tort law framework. We also noted that it is relatively simple to use this type of civil law as a method of regulating AI in a manner that is consistent across nations, and so avoid inconsistent regulation and race-to-the-bottom regulatory competition. Civil law provides two fundamental approaches to regulating harmful behavior: ex-ante and ex-post. Ex-ante interventions seek to prevent the behavior that gives rise to harm while ex-post liability retroactively punishes harmful conduct. The past decade has witnessed a shift toward preventative approaches to regulating information technologies to protect consumers from unsafe products.

Application of this well-intentioned philosophy to AI nevertheless does little to prevent harm, but it could hamper innovation. Given the nebulous definitions of AI and the rapid pace at which the field develops, ex-ante regulation presents lawmakers with the impossible task of predicting the trajectory of the AI industry. This challenge is compounded by the distributed and international nature of the AI development community. Considering these challenges, an ex-post liability regime that punishes AI misuse is likely to prove a more realistic and efficient path, as the world leaders in the Club de Madrid realized.

An approach that shifts the costs resulting from AI harms to manufacturers and thereby incentivizes the latter to deploy safe products and to self-regulate would be useful and could be achieved by the strict liability regime that has applied to products in the United States and elsewhere since the 1960s. Practically, this requires all AI deployments to keep easily accessible audit logs of actions they take, along with a liability regime that makes it easy to use these logs to assign liability.

If a strict liability regime were applied to AI, it would allow citizens and government to ensure citizen rights and mitigate harms. To implement this shift could require: (1) manufacturers and service providers to keep a detailed record of all decisions made by an AI (e.g., open audit trails, analogous to requiring companies to keep financial records); (2) creation of regulatory bodies (analogous to financial regulators) that are able to regularly audit these decision records in order to ensure citizen rights;

and (3) creation of trusts (analogous to credit unions) that are able to hold personal data for citizens, advocate for their rights, and aid them in litigation to mitigate harms.

EX-ANTE REGULATION IS WRONG FOR AI REGULATION

As jurisdictions around the world grapple with the challenge of formulating AI regulation, regulators seem drawn to the idea of creating a legal framework that ensures only "safe and trustworthy" AI enters the market. This regulatory approach betrays a fundamental misunderstanding about what AI is and who builds it.

Ex-ante regulation is, generally, a poor approach to AI regulation for three reasons. First, AI is a broad and evolving field that neither lends itself to one-size regulation nor permits accurate predictions about future developments. Second, AI development features low barriers to entry, which promotes a distributed and international AI development community and makes the enforcement of ex-ante regulation unrealistic. Ex-ante regulations not only fail to protect consumers but also needlessly hamper innovation. Finally, regulating the full spectrum of AI ex-ante across many different nations is inherently unrealistic.

Fundamentally, AI systems are a method of capturing patterns in data and utilizing the resulting insights; the term *artificial intelligence* captures systems ranging from relatively innocuous tax expert systems to facial recognition surveillance systems with far-reaching consequences. Like other broad categories of products, such as consumer goods, AI systems come in many shapes and sizes. However, the types of harm that they may cause and that we should seek to prevent are relatively easy to enumerate. Ex-ante regulation is misguided because it focuses on the complexity of AI systems and how they are developed rather than on the tractable set of possible harms these systems are capable of.

DESIGNING A FRAMEWORK FOR AI LIABILITY

For the reasons outlined above, attempts to use regulation to predict and prevent AI harms ex-ante are likely to be ineffective. A better solution would be to develop a legal framework grounded in tort law that draws on well-established, strict product liability principles and that also introduces incentives for AI creators to release safe products. The first step is to outline some key considerations for applying strict liability to AI.

Tort law provides a legal basis to shift losses associated with unsafe conduct from the injured party to the person causing the harm, thereby discouraging unsafe conduct. In most cases, to win in a tort suit, the injured party must demonstrate that the alleged tortfeasor acted negligently. However, in the case of product liability, US law generally applies the principle of strict liability, meaning that the injured party need only show that injuries arose from a product that was defective or falsely advertised.[2] Thus, applying the principles of strict liability to harms caused by AI creates effective incentives for AI manufacturers to release safe products.[3]

FINAL WORDS

This book has attempted to combine insights about the nature of human society with a deep understanding of technologies like digital media and AI in order to discover how humans and machines can best complement each other's abilities. Understanding which technologies we should use and for what purposes is critical for building better social institutions.

The first half of this book began by using a new computational sort of social science to better understand the key elements that produced the Enlightenment and other periods of great innovation. For example, the Enlightenment seems to have emerged from the combination of letter writing for sharing theories about the world, the mechanism of citing previous work so that you can identify theories that are widely accepted, and incentives for discovering valuable new theories. One fundamental insight is that humans are not rational individuals; rather, we are a communal, social species that builds knowledge through sharing stories, and our social institutions and technologies must fully leverage that reality. This better understanding suggests how to use AI to support human decision-making without diminishing human agency.

The insight that we are a communal species inspired the exploration in the second half of the book as to how we can build more agile, inclusive, and innovative social institutions by choosing appropriate, "community compatible" technology and cultural inventions. I also explored how to create more resilient, distributed organizations and how to adapt legal frameworks so that our social institutions remain responsive to human needs and current circumstances.

By choice, what the book has left undone is the creation of an action plan for how to build the right sorts of AI and the right sorts of institutions. That task should be done by consensus networks that include all stakeholders, not a single person or committee.

Earlier versions of AI have shown that this technology can be an important part of making our social institutions more efficient and responsive, but too often they have also made them less inclusive and more rigid by encouraging uniform rules and central control. The newest forms of AI, particularly GenAI, have even greater promise, but they also have the potential for causing even greater problems. This final chapter has argued that it is critical to keep a sharp eye on what these technologies are actually doing through open audit trails, strict liability, and civil law.

A particular concern is that regulation will likely be unsuccessful unless all major nations adopt similar, interoperable frameworks. This sort of interoperable global system already exists for international trade and internet governance. Since digital media and AI have worldwide reach already, we need a similar level of regulatory compatibility if we are to avoid companies moving operations to the least-regulated nations. We need to think about consensus solutions that will be supported by all major nations purely for their own selfish benefit if we are to avoid a race to the regulatory bottom.

Consensus organizations like the IETF, FATF, and WHO are good places to start developing a global AI and digital media ecosystem that is both safe and accountable. In order to handle regulation of AI in a way that keeps up with technological change, these consensus organizations now need to begin to include, at minimum, audit trails and liability rules for AI in their discussions. Over time we can see if stronger regulation is needed, but as the prime ministers and presidents of the Club de Madrid appreciated, this is a practical and immediate way to begin shaping AI while avoiding unforeseen side effects and existential dangers.

This last point, having the flexibility and ability to continually adapt, is particularly important for long-term challenges like climate change.

For long-term problems, the technologies, effects, and circumstances will continually change, and yet we need a sustained and coordinated effort. Such an effort is something that humanity has accomplished in only a few domains, such as commerce, health, and communications, and that was through the use of consensus organizations like the Uniform Law Commission or FATF. We should begin building better social institutions in partnership with these consensus organizations and work to evolve them to be more inclusive, distributed, and agile.

ACKNOWLEDGMENTS

I would like to particularly thank Tracy Heibeck for her critical feedback, encouragement, and diligent editing. As with my earlier books, she is a key contributor. I would also like to thank my network of collaborators, my team of students, and all the people who have invited me to participate in high-level policy discussions, senior management deliberations, and, of course, cutting-edge research seminars. Without these amazing collaborations and experiences, this book would not have been possible.

Finally, I would also like to thank the Project Liberty Institute and sponsors of the Stanford Digital Economy Lab and MIT Connection Science for their financial support and enthusiastic help in developing the ideas in this book. Without their support, much of the research reported here would have been impossible.

APPENDIX: PREDICTION IS HARD, ESPECIALLY ABOUT THE FUTURE

Western societies' institutions were created amid eighteenth- and nineteenth-century excitement about the mechanical model's success in industry, the natural sciences, and medicine. Inspired by these advances, leaders began thinking of society as akin to a complex mechanical device that could be analyzed by logic and reason in order to find the rules that would achieve their desired ends. Following the example that had worked so well in factories and in the armed forces, they built hierarchical institutions with strict rules so that individual discretion was limited and individuals were interchangeable, like gears in a machine.

For many decades, and in many countries, the model of society-as-machine worked much more reliably than the monarchies and warlords that the model replaced. But it has become clear that this mechanical approach to government, commerce, and social institutions is too rigid and unresponsive, too unconnected to people and circumstances, and lacks the creativity to overcome new challenges. Why?

OUR CHALLENGES ARE NOT EASILY PREDICTABLE

The central failure is that society, and the world in general, is not mechanical. Instead, it is constantly evolving, shaped by processes that occasionally combine in cascades that cause huge changes. Examples are viruses that are a constant low-level threat but occasionally cause a pandemic, weather that occasionally creates a tornado, or continental movements that sometimes create big earthquakes.

Just as physical cascades can destroy buildings, social cascades that change beliefs or norms of behavior can destroy social institutions. Examples of recent social cascades are market crashes, the adoption of smartphones for news, dating, and many other services, and many US residents moving out of cities in response to COVID. Just in the last decade or so, these cascades—people influencing each other, resulting in massive rapid change—have bankrupted businesses, decimated city centers, and drastically altered retail sales and local entertainment, to say nothing of people's jobs and career paths.

THE FOUR HORSEMEN OF SOCIAL FAILURE

In classical Western literature, the end of humanity comes at the hands of the Four Horsemen of the Apocalypse (Death, Famine, War, and Conquest). Analogously, cascades of behavior (e.g., fads and panics or collective behaviors that lead to overstressing our environment) can lead to the collapse of social institutions. I will call these behavioral cascades the "Four Horsemen of Social Failure": *unseen change, gray swans, one-size-fits-none decision-making*, and *myopia*. Our current social institutions, built on the model of society as a giant machine, are inadequate to adapt to these sorts of problems.

UNSEEN CHANGE

The first and most obvious difficulties faced by mechanical models are changes in factors that were once assumed to be constant. A current example is how the widespread adoption of working from home has changed the amount of office space a city needs. This has hurt city funding and threatens large changes in social programs and civic infrastructure. In almost all domains, we adopt policies and make investments as if the future will resemble the past, even though the phrase "past results do not guarantee future performance" is familiar to anyone who has put money into a US mutual fund or made a stock purchase.

If social changes happen slowly, over generations, then existing institutions have shown that they can adapt. When social changes are due to rapid cascades, however, our institutions' ability to adapt often comes up short. For instance, when COVID caused big businesses to go virtual, the people who were most hurt were the service and small business workers who kept city centers running, along with schoolchildren and people dependent on public services. Our social institutions were typically unable to adapt quickly enough to these new conditions.

Today, most businesses and governments are run on the principle of using the past to predict the future. Only recently have hedge funds and similar investment organizations begun to use sophisticated statistical tests to check for unanticipated change. Most of our society's institutions are designed with the assumption that conditions will not change rapidly, and so when their "ecological niche" changes, they often break. As a cautionary tale, many ancient civilizations collapsed when climate patterns changed and traditional patterns of food production deteriorated. Using the past as a guide to the future works—until it inevitably fails.

"GRAY SWANS," OR RARE EVENTS

An important way in which the past fails to predict the future is amid gray swans, or rare but unavoidable events. Rare events can often cause disasters because our social institutions were built to deal primarily with typical situations, and these systems do not recognize the inevitability of large, unpredictable events. Examples are forest fires, bank failures, and pandemics. Large, rare events can be categorized into two types: "black swans" and "gray swans." Black swan disasters are completely unanticipated events, such as the crop failures in Medieval Europe that were caused by volcano eruptions halfway around the world. Gray swan events are more familiar disasters such as hurricanes, plagues, or earthquakes, which we know are inevitable but for which the exact time and form are unpredictable.

Resilience and "anti-fragility" are ways to address these sorts of rare events—for instance, by stockpiling medicine or hedging currency—but aside from the expense of such preparations, we still need to experiment and learn in order to find new patterns of behavior that will work each time the environment changes. Each type of change can alter important factors, often unpredictably and sometimes in ways that we never suspected were important (e.g., people in the 1800s never thought about the effects of CO_2), and so we must experiment and learn to discover new methods and organizations that allow us to survive.

ONE SIZE FITS NONE

Another difficulty involved with making consistently good decisions comes from the fact that the experience of each individual or community may be very different compared to the average person's experience. In statistics, this is related to the technical term *nonergodicity*, which means the policies that seem to be good on average suffer from random factors (perhaps due to the other Four Horsemen) that can cause dramatic individual failures.[1] An example can make this clearer: imagine a coin toss where your wealth increases by 50 percent for heads but decreases by 40 percent for tails. Averaged across a large population, there will be exponential growth in wealth but more than half of the population will end up in poverty because their first few coin flips came up tails.

Investment bankers and venture capitalists are experts at this and try to get enough uncorrelated investments that they can be confident that the inevitable failures are more than compensated for by the few home-run investments. This problem is also unfortunately common when setting government policies. For instance, buying a house has been a major source of wealth creation for the average homeowner, but for people in communities affected by economic crashes, financial bubbles, or environmental changes, it has been a disaster.

Thinking of society in terms of a mechanical model downplays the effects of randomness: our experience with machines is that either things work or they are broken and must be fixed. Our social institutions typically select behaviors that are good for the average person, such as buying a home or getting a college education, and put in place incentives to encourage those behaviors. This oversimplifies the problem by implicitly assuming these policies will work for everyone. Perhaps the best way to control this sort of systematic oversimplification is through evidence and accountability. For instance, by keeping track of each policy's effects in each different community, essentially viewing the application of the policy to each community as an experiment, we can learn how to adapt policies so that they are most useful. Such community-by-community accountability was expensive when it was done by humans filling out paperwork; now, in the age of computers and digital accounting, it is nearly free.

MYOPIA

A final and even more basic problem with making consistently good decisions is myopia: the failure to consider all the factors that can drive change, instead focusing narrowly on a small handful of familiar variables. An example is the way that social policy is often analyzed only in terms of wealth and GDP, with factors such as life satisfaction and other social aspects neglected. The dangerous thing about myopia is that it applies both to our theory and reasoning as well as to our experimental methodology for developing scientific and reliable knowledge. Failure to include all the possible causal factors can be worse than a lack of theory or experimentation because it leads to false confidence in bad solutions.

For instance, in the fields of medicine and science, we are taught that experiments, known as randomized controlled experiments (RCTs), are the gold standard for reliably developing better policies, treatments, and insights. The idea of RCTs is to compare two examples that look identical except for one factor. For instance, evaluating two towns that have different educational systems but are otherwise similar allows us to isolate and measure the effect of the differences in their educational systems.

But all too often there is an unknown confounder: some unnoticed difference between the towns that accounts for different results (as seen in the Fragile Families Study), or the fact that the outcome being observed is inherently more variable than we assumed (e.g., it is subject to gray swan events, such as an unusual number of local businesses closing). For this reason, medicine and other scientific fields conduct meta-studies in which they survey a large number of RCT experiments to see how regularly the same result holds. But why would researchers do this if RCTs are the "gold standard"? It is because they recognize that RCTs are typically done in one carefully controlled environment, and thus the experimental results can be due to the special circumstances of that experiment. Similar experiments in many different contexts are needed to be confident that the results are generally trustworthy.[2] Furthermore, experiments to test how treatments and health policies work in many different contexts produce a community intelligence that can make more effective and reliable decisions.

THE MECHANICAL MODEL LIMITS REASON

The Four Horsemen problems happen in almost all human endeavors. This means that it is often arrogance and folly to assume, as is typical of the mechanical model mindset, that we have all the relevant facts and can reason through enormously complex situations. Our culture tends to glorify logic and deductive reasoning, but without a solid real-world trial and continuous monitoring of outcomes, logic and reason often fail.

Instead, we need to adopt a different, more humble approach—that of continuously trying new approaches, keeping track of potentially influential factors, and trying to discover when policies work and when they do not. This is the approach known as abductive reasoning. Facts and deductive reasoning are still of use, of course, but mainly to guide what experiments to try and in trying to draw conclusions from them. Reason is no longer the central player; instead, data from experiments are the guiding light. And, as medical researchers know, we need many experiments in different environments to be confident of the result.

This is, of course, exactly the day-to-day practice of science, even though researchers like to highlight their big equations and complex deductions. Even in fields as well understood as mechanical design, engineers still build and test models. In medicine, researchers continue to spend billions of dollars testing new drugs on large test populations. Theory is useful to make hypotheses, but experimental results rule because each instance may be subtly but importantly different.

Societies today are complex and change fluidly as they respond to new influences, quite the opposite of the mechanical model, and so figuring out what works best for a particular community is very hard because the Four Horsemen problems—unseen change, rare events, one-size-fits-none, and myopia—are prominent. To improve our social institutions we need hundreds if not thousands of communities that are all simultaneously trying different strategies (e.g., running different experiments) to learn how to best adapt to their particular set of problems and opportunities. By sharing the stories of what each community did, how it worked out, and what the unintended consequences were, we can dramatically enhance our community intelligence.

The prevailing mechanical approach to policymaking fails in these situations because the facts change and we do not have good ways of knowing which facts are changing or how to notice them beginning to change. A cooperative story-sharing approach addresses this because it is continually asking if our understanding of how the system behaves is still valid. Both the mathematics of cooperative decision-making and the history of experimental science show that our best chance to be able to deal with the Four Horsemen of Social Failure is by employing cooperative story sharing to search for solutions. Many experiments in many different communities are required to be confident that a solution is sufficiently general to be applied widely.

NOTES

CHAPTER 1

1. Kirsty E. Graham and Catherine Hobaiter, "Towards a Great Ape Dictionary: Inexperienced Humans Understand Common Nonhuman Ape Gestures," *PLOS Biology* 21, no. 1 (2023): e3001939, https://doi.org/10.1371/journal.pbio.3001939; Wikipedia, "Pant-hoot," last modified October 2023, https://en.m.wikipedia.org/wiki/Pant-hoot; Joseph Henrich, *The Secret of Our Success: How Culture Is Driving Human Evolution, Domesticating Our Species, and Making Us Smarter* (Princeton, NJ: Princeton University Press, 2015).

2. B. David et al., "Archaeological Evidence of an Ethnographically Documented Australian Aboriginal Ritual Dated to the Last Ice Age," *Nature Human Behaviour* 8 (2024): 1481–1492, https://doi.org/10.1038/s41562-024-01912-w; Patrick D. Nunn and Nicholas J. Reid, "Aboriginal Memories of Inundation of the Australian Coast Dating from More than 7000 Years Ago," *Australian Geographer* 47, no. 1 (2016): 11–47, https://doi.org/10.1080/00049182.2015.1077539.

3. *Oxford English Dictionary*, "intelligence," accessed January 14, 2025, https://www.oed.com/dictionary/intelligence_n?tab=meaning_and_use#214347.

4. *Oxford English Dictionary*, "wisdom," accessed January 14, 2025, https://www.oed.com/dictionary/wisdom_n?tab=meaning_and_use#14117686.

5. Abdullah Almaatouq et al., "Adaptive Social Networks Promote the Wisdom of Crowds," *Proceedings of the National Academy of Sciences of the United States of America* 117, no. 21 (2020): 11379–11386, https://doi.org/10.1073/pnas.1917687117.

6. Wikipedia, "Abductive Reasoning," last modified January 2, 2025, https://en.wikipedia.org/wiki/Abductive_reasoning.

7. *Oxford English Dictionary*, "story," accessed January 14, 2025, https://www.oed.com/dictionary/story_n?tab=meaning_and_use#20448297.

8. Hang Jiang et al., "Leveraging Large Language Models for Learning Complex Legal Concepts through Storytelling," in *ACL Anthology* (Bangkok: ACL, 2024), 7194–7219, https://aclanthology.org/2024.acl-long.388/.

9. S. Neuman, "1 in 4 Americans Thinks the Sun Goes Around the Earth, Survey Says," NPR, February 14, 2014, https://www.npr.org/sections/thetwo-way/2014/02/14/277058739/1-in-4-americans-think-the-sun-goes-around-the-earth-survey-says.

10. Abdullah Almaatouq et al., "Beyond Playing 20 Questions with Nature: Integrative Experiment Design in the Social and Behavioral Sciences," *Behavioral and Brain Sciences* 47 (2022): e33, https://doi:10.1017/S0140525X22002874.

11. Henrich, *The Secret of Our Success*.

12. Michelle Vaccaro et al., "When Combinations of Humans and AI Are Useful: A Systematic Review and Meta-Analysis," preprint, arXiv, last updated October 29, 2024, https://arxiv.org/abs/2405.06087.

13. Anita Williams Woolley et al., "Evidence for a Collective Intelligence Factor in the Performance of Human Groups," *Science* 330, no. 6004 (2010): 686–688, https://doi.org/10.1126/science.1193147.

14. E. L. Glaeser and C. David, *Survival of the City: Living and Thriving in an Age of Isolation* (New York: Penguin, 2022).

15. "Data Provenance Initiative," MIT Connection Science, accessed January 14, 2025, https://transformers.mit.edu.

16. Adam Smith, *The Theory of Moral Sentiments* (London: A. Miller, 1759).

17. Or more accurately, the English and Chinese speaking portions of humanity. Woolley et al., "Evidence for a Collective Intelligence Factor"; Almaatouq et al., "Adaptive Social Networks Promote the Wisdom of Crowds."

18. Mohammad Atari et al., "Which Humans?," preprint, PsyArXiv, last edited June 20, 2024, https://osf.io/preprints/psyarxiv/5b26t; T. H. Costello et al., "Durably Reducing Conspiracy Beliefs Through Dialogues with AI," *Science* 385, no. 6714 (2024), https://www.science.org/doi/10.1126/science.adq1814.

19. Alex Pentland, *Social Physics: How Social Networks Can Make Us Smarter* (New York: Penguin Press, 2014); Henrich, *The Secret of Our Success*.

20. Wikipedia, "Past Sea Level," last modified January 6, 2025, https://en.wikipedia.org/wiki/Past_sea_level. It is interesting to note that seas rose faster than mean projections due to climate change (2.5 meters per century). Since human civilizations have always been built on waterways and seacoasts, this likely destroyed any civilization older than 14,500 years.

21. J. C. R. Licklider, "Man-Computer Symbiosis," *IRE Transactions on Human Factors in Electronics*, vol. HFE-1 (March 1960): 4–11.

22. J. Wai et al., "The Most Successful and Influential Americans Come from a Surprisingly Narrow Range of 'Elite' Educational Backgrounds," *Humanities and Social Sciences Communications* 11, no. 1129 (September 2024), https://doi.org/10.1057/s41599-024-03547-8.

23. Emily Velasco, "Artificial Intelligence Is Key to Better Climate Models, Say Researchers," Caltech, October 10, 2023, https://www.caltech.edu/about/news/artificial-intelligence-is-key-to-better-climate-models-say-researchers; Matthew Chun, "How Artificial Intelligence Is Revolutionizing Drug Discovery," Bill of Health, Harvard Law, accessed January 14, 2025, https://blog.petrieflom.law.harvard.edu/2023/03/20/how-artificial-intelligence-is-revolutionizing-drug-discovery/; Hang Jiang et al.,

"Leveraging Large Language Models for Learning Complex Legal Concepts Through Storytelling," *ACL Anthology* (2024): 7194–7219, https://aclanthology.org/2024.acl-long.388/.

24. Lily L. Tsai et al., "Generative AI for Pro-democracy Platforms," March 2024, https://mit-genai.pubpub.org/pub/mn45hexw/release/1.

25. For readers with a mathematical background in distributed decision-making, I will mention that it is a self-configuring network for sharing action-reward observations among cooperating multi-arm Bayesian agents in order to optimally minimize regret for both individual and group fitness. The value added by the community intelligence perspective comes from showing the mathematical, estimation-theoretic basis for how these cultural inventions improve human decision-making at the individual, organizational, and societal scales.

CHAPTER 2

1. Wikipedia, "Songline," November 9, 2024, https://en.wikipedia.org/wiki/Songline.

2. Bruno David et al., "Archaeological Evidence of an Ethnographically Documented Australian Aboriginal Ritual Dated to the Last Ice Age," *Nature Human Behavior* 8 (July 2024): 1481–1492, https://doi.org/10.1038/s41562-024-01912-w; Patrick D. Nunn and Nicholas J. Reid, "Aboriginal Memories of Inundation of the Australian Coast Dating from More Than 7000 Years Ago," *Australian Geographer* 47, no. 1 (2016): 11–47, https://doi.org/10.1080/00049182.2015.1077539.

3. Philip N. Johnson-Laird, "Mental Models and Human Reasoning," *Proceedings of the National Academy of Sciences of the United States of America* 107, no. 43 (2010): 18243–18250, https://doi.org/10.1073/pnas.1012933107.

4. P. M. Krafft et al., "Bayesian Collective Learning Emerges from Heuristic Social Learning," *Cognition* 212 (July 2021), https://doi.org/10.1016/j.cognition.2020.104469; Abdullah Almaatouq et al., "Adaptive Social Networks Promote the Wisdom of Crowds," *Proceedings of the National Academy of Sciences of the United States of America* 117, no. 21 (2022): 11379–11386, https://doi.org/10.1073/pnas.1917687117; Pawel Fedurek et al., "Sequential Information in a Great Ape Utterance," *Scientific Reports* 6, no. 38226 (2016), https://doi.org/10.1038/srep38226.

5. Wikipedia, "Waggle Dance," January 14, 2025, https://en.wikipedia.org/wiki/Waggle_dance.

6. Almaatouq et al., "Adaptive Social Networks Promote the Wisdom of Crowds."

7. Anita Williams Woolley et al., "Evidence for a Collective Intelligence Factor in the Performance of Human Groups," *Science* 330, no. 6004 (September 2010): 686–688, https://doi.org/10.1126/science.1193147.

8. Deborah. G. Ancona and Henrik Bresman, *X-teams: How to Build Teams That Lead, Innovate, and Succeed* (Cambridge, MA: Harvard Business Press, 2007); Stanley McChrystal et al., *Team of Teams: New Rules of Engagement for a Complex World* (New York: Penguin, 2015).

9. Daniel Kahneman, *Thinking, Fast and Slow* (New York: Farrar, Straus and Giroux, 2011).

10. Kahneman, *Thinking, Fast and Slow*.

11. Abhimanyu Dubey and Alex Pentland, "Cooperative Multi-agent Bandits with Heavy Tails," *International Conference on Machine Learning*, no. 256 (2020): 2730–2739, https://dl.acm.org/doi/10.5555/3524938.3525194.

12. Abhimanyu Dubey and Alex Pentland, "Kernel Methods for Cooperative Multi-agent Contextual Bandits," *Proceedings of the 37th International Conference on Machine Learning*, no. 257 (2020): 2740–2750, https://dl.acm.org/doi/abs/10.5555/3524938.3525195.

13. Krafft et al., "Bayesian Collective Learning Emerges."

14. Alex Pentland, "Beyond the Echo Chamber," *Harvard Business Review*, November 2013, https://hbr.org/2013/11/beyond-the-echo-chamber.

15. Dhaval Adjodah et al., "Accuracy-Risk Trade-Off due to Social Learning in Crowd-Sourced Financial Predictions," *Entropy* 23, no. 7 (2021): 801, https://doi.org/10.3390/e23070801.

16. Michelle Vaccaro et al., "When Are Combinations of Humans and AI Useful?," preprint, arXiv, last updated May 8, 2024, https://arxiv.org/html/2405.06087v1.

17. Tobin South et al., "Building a Healthier Feed: Private Location Trace Intersection Driven Feed Recommendations," *International Conference on Social Computing, Behavioral-Cultural Modeling and Prediction and Behavior Representation in Modeling and Simulation* (2023): 54–63, https://doi.org/10.1007/978-3-031-43129-6_6.

18. Guy Zyskind et al., "Don't Forget Private Retrieval: Distributed Private Similarity Search for Large Language Models," preprint, arXiv, last updated November 21, 2023, https://doi.org/10.48550/arXiv.2311.12955.

19. "Data Provenance Initiative," MIT Connection Science, accessed January 14, 2025, https://transformers.mit.edu.

20. Chloe Taylor, "Bill Gates Predicts Everyone Will Have an AI-Powered Personal Assistant Within 5 Years—Whether They Work in an Office or Not: 'They Will Utterly Change How We Live,'" Yahoo Finance, November 10, 2023, https://finance.yahoo.com/news/bill-gates-predicts-everyone-ai-125827903.html.

CHAPTER 3

1. Edward Glaeser, *Triumph of the City: How Our Greatest Invention Makes Us Richer, Smarter, Greener, Healthier, and Happier* (New York: Penguin, 2012); Ronald S. Burt, "The Network Structure of Social Capital," *Research in Organizational Behavior* 22 (2000): 345–423, https://doi.org/10.1016/S0191-3085(00)22009-1; Mark S. Granovetter, "The Strength of Weak Ties," *American Journal of Sociology* 78, no. 6 (1973): 1360–1380, https://www.jstor.org/stable/2776392; Nathan Eagle et al., "Network Diversity and Economic Development," *Science* 328, no. 5981 (2010): 1029–1031, https://www.science.org/doi/abs/10.1126/science.1186605.

2. Glaeser, *Triumph of the City*.

3. Glaeser, *Triumph of the City*.

4. Xiaowen Dong et al., "Social Bridges in Urban Purchase Behavior," *ACM Transactions on Intelligent Systems and Technology* 9, no. 3 (2017): 1–29, https://dl.acm.org/doi/10.1145/3149409.

5. Wei Pan et al., "Urban Characteristics Attributable to Density-Driven Tie Formation," *Nature Communications* 4, no. 1961 (2013), https://doi.org/10.1038/ncomms2961.

6. David Holtz et al., "Interdependence and the Cost of Uncoordinated Responses to COVID-19," *Proceedings of the National Academy of Sciences of the United States of America* 117, no. 33 (2020): 19837–19843, https://doi.org/10.1073/pnas.2009522117.

7. Yuan Yuan et al., "Implications of COVID-19 Vaccination Heterogeneity in Mobility Networks," *Communications Physics* 6, no. 206 (2023), https://doi.org/10.1038/s42005-023-01325-7.

8. Takahiro Yabe et al., "Understanding Post-disaster Population Recovery Patterns," *Journal of the Royal Society Interface* 17, no. 163 (2020): 20190532, https://doi.org/10.1098/rsif.2019.0532.

9. "SMART Launches Research Group to Advance AI, Automation, and the Future of Work," MIT News, August 23, 2023, https://news.mit.edu/2023/smart-launches-m3s-research-group-advance-ai-automation-future-work-0823.

10. Matthew J. Salganik et al., "Measuring the Predictability of Life Outcomes with a Scientific Mass Collaboration," *Proceedings of the National Academy of Sciences of the United States of America* 117, no. 15 (2020): 8398–8403, https://doi.org/10.1073/pnas.1915006117.

11. "Media Lab Team Tops Fragile Families Challenge," MIT News, October 4, 2017, http://news.mit.edu/2017/mit-human-dynamics-team-tops-fragile-families-challenge-1004.

12. "Neighborhoods Matter," Opportunity Insights, accessed January 14, 2025, https://opportunityinsights.org/neighborhoods/.

13. Shi Kai Chong et al., "Economic Outcomes Predicted by Diversity in Cities," *EPJ Data Science* 9, no. 17 (2020), https://doi.org/10.1140/epjds/s13688-020-00234-x.

14. Pan et al., "Urban Characteristics Attributable to Density-Driven Tie Formation."

15. Raj Chetty et al., "Social Capital I: Measurement and Associations with Economic Mobility," *Nature* 608, no. 7921 (2022): 108–121, https://doi.org/10.1038/s41586-022-04996-4; Raj Chetty et al., "Social Capital II: Determinants of Economic Connectedness," *Nature* 608, no. 7921 (2022): 122–134, https://doi.org/10.1038/s41586-022-04997-3.

16. Nicholas S. Caros, "Preparing Urban Mobility for the Future of Work" (PhD diss., MIT, 2023), https://www.researchgate.net/publication/357619016_Preparing_urban_mobility_for_the_future_of_work.

17. Zhuangyuan Fan et al., "Diversity Beyond Density: Experienced Social Mixing of Urban Streets," *PNAS Nexus* 2, no. 4 (April 2023): pgad077, https://doi.org/10.1093/pnasnexus/pgad077.

18. Alexandra Cass, "Why Coffee Has Been Banned Throughout History," Mashed, November 3, 2021, https://www.mashed.com/650885/why-coffee-has-been-banned-throughout-history/.

19. Yuan Yuan et al., "Research on the Relationship Between Entrepreneurship Diversity and Performance of Regional Innovation Networks—Micro Data Analysis Based on 3255 Chinese Incubators," *Theory & Practice*, no. 9 (2017): 152–155.

20. Robert J. Sampson et al., "Neighborhoods and Violent Crime: A Multilevel Study of Collective Efficacy," *Science* 277, no. 5328 (1997): 918–924, https://www.science.org/doi/10.1126/science.277.5328.918; Shi Kai Chong et al., "Economic Outcomes Predicted by Diversity in Cities," *EPJ Data Science* 9, no. 17 (2020), https://doi.org/10.1140/epjds/s13688-020-00234-x.

21. Robert J. Sampson and Brian L. Levy, "The Enduring Neighborhood Effect, Everyday Urban Mobility, and Violence in Chicago," *University of Chicago Law Review* 89, no. 2 (2022): 323–348, https://www.jstor.org/stable/27132253.

22. Alia Braley et al., "Why Voters Who Value Democracy Participate in Democratic Backsliding," *Nature Human Behaviour* 7, no. 8 (2023): 1282–1293, https://www.nature.com/articles/s41562-023-01594-w.

23. James Fishkin et al., "Is Deliberation an Antidote to Extreme Partisan Polarization? Reflections on 'America in One Room,'" *American Political Science Review* 115, no. 4 (2021): 1464–1481, https://doi.org/10.1017/S0003055421000642.

24. Jan G. Voelkel et al., "Megastudy Identifying Effective Interventions to Strengthen Americans' Democratic Attitudes," preprint, OSF Preprints, last edited March 25, 2025, https://doi.org/10.31219/osf.io/y79u5.

25. Jens Ludwig et al., "Urban Poverty and Juvenile Crime: Evidence from a Randomized Housing-Mobility Experiment," *Quarterly Journal of Economics* 116, no. 2 (May 2001): 655–679, https://doi.org/10.1162/00335530151144122; Sampson et al., "Neighborhoods and Violent Crime."

26. Abdullah Almaatouq et al., "Are You Your Friends' Friend? Poor Perception of Friendship Ties Limits the Ability to Promote Behavioral Change," *PloS One* 11, no. 3 (2016): e0151588, https://doi.org/10.1371/journal.pone.0151588.

27. Yves-Alexandre de Montjoye et al., "The Strength of the Strongest Ties in Collaborative Problem Solving," *Scientific Reports* 4, no. 5277 (2014), https://doi.org/10.1038/srep05277.

28. Esteban Moro et al., "Mobility Patterns Are Associated with Experienced Income Segregation in Large US Cities," *Nature Communications* 12, no. 4633 (2021), https://doi.org/10.1038/s41467-021-24899-8.

29. Sandro Lera et al., "Prediction and Prevention of Disproportionally Dominant Agents in Complex Networks," *Proceedings of the National Academy of Sciences of the*

United States of America 117, no. 44 (2020): 27090–27095, https://doi.org/10.1073/pnas.2003632117.

30. Robert Mahari et al., "Time for a New Antitrust Era: Refocusing Antitrust Law to Invigorate Competition in the 21st Century," *Stanford Computational Antitrust* 1, no. 52 (2021), https://ssrn.com/abstract=3943548.

31. Michael Bühler et al., "Harnessing Digital Federation Platforms and Data Cooperatives to Empower SMEs and Local Small Communities," G20 Meeting (2023), https://t20ind.org/research/harnessing-digital-federation-platforms/.

32. Tobin South et al., "Building a Healthier Feed: Private Location Trace Intersection Driven Feed Recommendations," in *International Conference on Social Computing, Behavioral-Cultural Modeling and Prediction and Behavior Representation in Modeling and Simulation* (Cham: Springer Nature Switzerland, 2023), 54–63, https://doi.org/10.1007/978-3-031-43129-6_6; see also https://transformers.mit.edu.

CHAPTER 4

1. Daniel Carmody et al., "The Effect of Co-location on Human Communication Networks," *Nature Computational Science* 2, no. 8 (2022): 494–503, https://pubmed.ncbi.nlm.nih.gov/38177800/.

2. Till Johannes Hartmann and Carlos Feyreyra, "What Are the Costs of Corruption?," *Governance for Development* (World Bank Blogs), December 22, 2022, https://blogs.worldbank.org/en/governance/what-are-costs-corruption.

3. Timothy A. Judge and Daniel M. Cable, "The Effect of Physical Height on Workplace Success and Income: Preliminary Test of a Theoretical Model," *Journal of Applied Psychology* 89, no. 3 (2004): 428–441, https://pubmed.ncbi.nlm.nih.gov/15161403/.

4. Editors of journals generally only decide if manuscripts are relevant to their community. They don't decide which content is best.

5. Dashun Wang and Albert-László Barabási, *The Science of Science* (Cambridge University Press, 2021).

6. Sadamori Kojaku et al., "Uncovering the Universal Dynamics of Citation Systems: From Science of Science to Law of Law and Patterns of Patents," paper presented at the International School and Conference on Network Science, Vienna, Austria, July 2023.

7. However, the current review mechanisms are seriously compromised by overreliance on features of the authors and lack of investigative resources.

8. A. Ciannameo et al., "Bottom-Up Approach to Set Research Needs in Healthcare," *European Journal of Public Health* 33, no. S2 (2023): ckad160–1646, https://doi.org/10.1093/eurpub/ckad160.1646.

9. Georg von Krogh and Sebastian Spaeth, "The Open Source Software Phenomenon: Characteristics That Promote Research," *Journal of Strategic Information Systems* 16, no. 3 (2007): 236–253, https://doi.org/10.1016/j.jsis.2007.06.001.

10. "Better Laws," Uniform Law Commission, accessed January 14, 2025, https://uniformlaws.org.

CHAPTER 5

1. Alex Pentland and Patrick Davis, "How Decentralized Systems Can Help Rebuild Local Communities," World Economic Forum Fourth Industrial Revolution, 2021, https://www.weforum.org/agenda/2021/10/how-decentralized-systems-can-help-rebuild-local-communities/.

2. Shoshona Zuboff, *The Age of Surveillance Capitalism* (London: Profile Books, 2019).

3. Alex Pentland, "Reality Mining of Mobile Communications: Toward a New Deal on Data," in *The Global Information Technology Report 2009–2009: Mobility in a Networked World*, ed. Soumitre Dutta and Irene Mia (Geneva: World Economic Forum, 2009), https://hd.media.mit.edu/wef_globalit.pdf.

4. Sandro Lera et al., "Prediction and Prevention of Disproportionally Dominant Agents in Complex Networks," *Proceedings of the National Academy of Sciences of the United States of America* 117, no. 44 (2020): 27090–27095, https://doi.org/10.1073/pnas.2003632117.

5. Lera et al., "Prediction and Prevention of Disproportionally Dominant Agents."

6. Yann LeCun (@ylecun), "LLMx can plan, eh?," X, June 21, 2024, 12:06 p.m., retweet of @colin_fraser, https://x.com/ylecun/status/1804184085125857687?lang=en. Because people are writing about Yann's story online, some of the more updated large language models can now "solve" this trivial problem.

7. Lera et al., "Prediction and Prevention of Disproportionally Dominant Agents."

8. Robert Mahari et al., "Time for a New Antitrust Era: Refocusing Antitrust Law to Invigorate Competition in the 21st Century," *Stanford Computational Antitrust* 1 (2021): 52, https://ssrn.com/abstract=3943548.

CHAPTER 6

1. Wikipedia, "The WELL," last updated November 3, 2024, https://en.wikipedia.org/wiki/The_WELL.

2. Alex Pentland and Lily Tsai, "Toward Building Deliberative Digital Media: From Subversion to Consensus," *PNAS Nexus* 3, no. 10 (October 2024): 407, https://doi.org/10.1093/pnasnexus/pgae407.

3. Lisa P. Argyle et al., "Leveraging AI for Democratic Discourse: Chat Interventions Can Improve Online Political Conversations at Scale," *Proceedings of the National Academy of Sciences of the United States of America* 120, no. 41 (2023): e2311627120, https://doi.org/10.1073/pnas.231162712.

4. Scott Neuman, "1 in 4 Americans Thinks the Sun Goes Around the Earth, Survey Says," NPR, February 14, 2014, https://www.npr.org/sections/thetwo-way/2014/02/14/277058739/1-in-4-americans-think-the-sun-goes-around-the-earth-survey-says; Peter Andre et al., "Globally Representative Evidence on the Actual and Perceived Support for Climate Action," *Nature Climate Change* 14 (2024): 253–259, https://doi.org/10.1038/s41558-024-01925-3.

5. Soroush Vosoughi et al., "The Spread of True and False News Online," *Science* 359, no. 6380 (2018): 1146–1151, https://www.science.org/doi/10.1126/science.aap9559.

6. Gordon Pennycook and David G. Rand, "Accuracy Prompts Are a Replicable and Generalizable Approach for Reducing the Spread of Misinformation," *Nature Communications* 13, no. 2333 (2022), https://www.nature.com/articles/s41467-022-30073-5.

7. Ziv Epstein, "The Dynamics of Attention in Digital Ecosystems" (PhD diss., MIT, 2023), https://dspace.mit.edu/handle/1721.1/152002.

8. Daniel Kahneman, *Thinking, Fast and Slow* (New York: Farrar, Straus and Giroux, 2011).

9. Pentland and Tsai, "Toward Building Deliberative Digital Media."

10. Raymond La Raja and Brian F. Schaffner, "A Cash Lottery Increases Voter Turnout," *PloS One* 17 no. 6 (2022), https://doi.org/10.1371/journal.pone.0268640.

11. Kenneth J. Arrow et al., "The Promise of Prediction Markets," *Science* 320, no. 5878 (2008): 877–878, https://www.science.org/doi/10.1126/science.1157679.

12. Ankur Mani et al., "Inducing Peer Pressure to Promote Cooperation," *Scientific Reports* 3, no. 1735 (2013), https://doi.org/10.1038/srep01735.

13. Yuan Yuan et al., "Gift Contagion in Online Groups: Evidence from Virtual Red Packets," *Management Science* 70, no. 7 (2024): 4465–4479, https://doi.org/10.1287/mnsc.2023.4906.

14. Chris Horton, "A Simple but Ingenious System Taiwan Uses to Crowdsource Its Laws," *MIT Technology Review*, August 21, 2018, https://www.technologyreview.com/2018/08/21/240284/the-simple-but-ingenious-system-taiwan-uses-to-crowdsource-its-laws/.

15. Sandro Lera et al., "Prediction and Prevention of Disproportionally Dominant Agents in Complex Networks," *Proceedings of the National Academy of Sciences of the United States of America* 117, no. 44 (2020): 27090–27095, https://doi.org/10.1073/pnas.2003632117.

16. Abdullah Almaatouq et al., "Adaptive Social Networks Promote the Wisdom of Crowds," *Proceedings of the National Academy of Sciences of the United States of America* 117, no. 21 (2020): 11379–11386, https://doi.org/10.1073/pnas.1917687117.

17. Dhaval Adjodah et al., "Accuracy-Risk Trade-Off Due to Social Learning in Crowd-Sourced Financial Predictions," *Entropy* 23, no. 7 (2021): 801, https://doi.org/10.3390/e23070801.

18. Horton, "A Simple but Ingenious System Taiwan Uses to Crowdsource Its Laws."

19. Adjodah et al., "Accuracy-Risk Trade-Off"; P. M. Krafft et al., "Bayesian Collective Learning Emerges from Heuristic Social Learning," *Cognition* 212 (July 2021), https://doi.org/10.1016/j.cognition.2020.104469; Alia Braley et al., "The Subversion Dilemma: Why Voters Who Cherish Democracy Participate in Democratic Backsliding," *Nature Human Behaviour* (2022), https://osf.io/my987/; and Almaatouq et al., "Adaptive Social Networks Promote the Wisdom of Crowds."

20. "MIT Scholars Awarded Seed Grants to Probe the Social Implications of Generative AI," *MIT News*, September 18, 2023, https://news.mit.edu/2023/mit-scholars-awarded-seed-grants-generative-ai-0918.

21. Michiel Bakker et al., "Fine-Tuning Language Models to Find Agreement Among Humans with Diverse Preferences," *Advances in Neural Information Processing Systems* 35 (2022): 38176–38189, https://doi.org/10.48550/arXiv.2211.15006.

22. Sadamori Kojaku et al., "Uncovering the Universal Dynamics of Citation Systems: From Science of Science to Law of Law and Patterns of Patents," paper presented at the International School and Conference on Network Science, Vienna, Austria, July 2023, https://arxiv.org/html/2501.15552v1.

23. Pentland and Tsai, "Toward Building Deliberative Digital Media."

CHAPTER 7

1. Stanley McChrystal et al., *Team of Teams: New Rules of Engagement for a Complex World* (New York: Penguin, 2015).

2. Alex Pentland, *Social Physics: How Social Networks Can Make Us Smarter* (New York: Penguin, 2015).

3. Andrew McAfee, *The Geek Way: The Radical Mindset That Drives Extraordinary Results* (New York: Little Brown, 2023).

4. Uniform Law Commission, "Better Laws," accessed January 14, 2025, https://uniformlaws.org.

5. Elinor Ostrom, *Governing the Commons: The Evolution of Institutions for Collective Action* (Cambridge: Cambridge University Press, 1990).

6. Wikipedia, "Quality Circle," last updated January 7, 2025, https://en.wikipedia.org/wiki/Quality_circle.

7. Data Revolution Group, "Data Revolution Report," published for United Nations Secretary-General by the Independent Expert Advisory Group on a Data Revolution for Sustainable Development, November 2014, https://www.undatarevolution.org/report/.

8. Data Revolution Group, "Data Revolution Report"; Data-Pop Alliance, "We Want to Change the World with Data," accessed on January 14, 2025, https://datapopalliance.org/about/about-dpa/.

9. Abhijit V. Banerjee and Esther Duflo, *Poor Economics: A Radical Rethinking of the Way to Fight Global Poverty* (New York: PublicAffairs Publishing, 2011).

10. "The Atlas of Economic Complexity," Harvard Growth Lab, accessed on January 14, 2025, https://atlas.cid.harvard.edu/; "The World Factbook," CIA, accessed on January 14, 2025, https://www.cia.gov/the-world-factbook/.

11. "FRED Economic Data," Federal Reserve Bank of St. Louis, accessed on January 14, 2025, https://fred.stlouisfed.org/; Phil Gramm et al., *The Myth of American Inequality: How Government Biases Policy Debate* (Rowman & Littlefield, 2024); Wikipedia, "Social Services," last updated February 10, 2025, https://en.wikipedia.org/wiki/Social_services.

12. Alex Pentland et al., *Building the New Economy: Data as Capital* (Cambridge, MA: MIT Press, 2021).

13. Michiel Bakker et al., "Fine-Tuning Language Models to Find Agreement Among Humans with Diverse Preferences," *Advances in Neural Information Processing Systems* 35 (2022): 38176–38189, https://arxiv.org/abs/2211.15006.

14. Anthony Bryk et al., "Policy Lessons from Chicago's Experience with Decentralization," *Brookings Papers on Education Policy* 2 (1999): 67–127, https://www.jstor.org/stable/20067207; Adam Bychawski, "How the Tories Drove Britain's Local Services into Bankruptcy," *Open Democracy*, February 29, 2024, https://www.opendemocracy.net/en/council-cuts-austerity-tories-bankrupt-youth-services-sure-start-school-nurses/.

15. Alia Braley et al., "Why Voters Who Value Democracy Participate in Democratic Backsliding," *Nature Human Behaviour* 7, no. 8 (2023): 1282–1293, https://www.nature.com/articles/s41562-023-01594-w.

16. "Public Trust in Government: 1958–2024," Pew Research Center, January 14, 2025, https://www.pewresearch.org/politics/2024/06/24/public-trust-in-government-1958-2024/.

17. Pentland et al., *Building the New Economy*.

18. Michael Bühler et al., "Harnessing Digital Federation Platforms and Data Cooperatives to Empower SMEs and Local Small Communities," G20 Meeting (2023), https://t20ind.org/research/harnessing-digital-federation-platforms/.

19. "India Stack Is . . ." India Stack, accessed on January 14, 2025, https://indiastack.org/.

20. "India Shares Citizen Stack," Citizen Stack, accessed January 14, 2025, https://www.citizenstack.world/.

CHAPTER 8

1. One might ask about the COP climate change process, which appears to be a consensus network that has raised awareness of climate change and secured political promises but has seemingly had relatively little real-world success. Perhaps the real problem is that the COP process has not included all of the stakeholders affected by changes in energy policy. As Elinor Ostrom argued, commons must be governed by all stakeholders.

2. Under a strict product liability regime, manufacturers are liable for harms to persons or property caused by defects in the products they sell, where a defect may be a manufacturing or design defect or failure to warn consumers.

3. Causation: AI systems are often criticized for their lack of explainability, and this shortcoming may make it challenging to determine when a defective AI system has *caused* a harm. While concerns over AI explainability are sometimes exaggerated—after all, human decision-making is hardly a fully explainable process—a lack of explainability may obscure defects and make causation difficult to pin down.

However, in most cases, it may be enough to compare the AI system to a baseline (i.e., a human or another AI) to determine whether the baseline system would likely have given rise to the same harm. To enable such ex-post algorithmic auditing, AI manufactures will, at the very least, need to maintain anonymized records of input data and model outputs that can be analyzed during trial.

Maintenance of input and output data is key to both harm mitigation and vigilance against harm by use of continuous audit. To avoid litigation and improve performance, companies would want to continuously check their performance internally, much like balancing the books each night, but they would also be subject to regular outside audit and audit during trial discovery.

Damages: Another challenge that must be resolved to effectively apply the strict liability framework to AI is the assessment of damages. For this reason, it may make sense to expand strict liability for AI to also include economic losses when they are caused by an AI system and there was no contractual relationship between the injured party and the manufacturer.

Finally, a comprehensive AI liability framework may require the definition of statutory damages to capture additional harms such as loss of privacy to ultimately incentivize AI manufactures to bear them in mind as they deploy their products.

APPENDIX

1. Wikipedia, "Ergodicity," last updated February 6, 2025, https://en.wikipedia.org/wiki/Ergodicity#.

2. Anna-Bettina Haidich, "Meta-analysis in Medical Research," *Hippokratia* 14, no. S1 (2010): 29–37, https://pmc.ncbi.nlm.nih.gov/articles/PMC3049418/.

INDEX

Abductive reasoning, 6, 18, 142
Adjodah, Dhaval, 29
Ahn, Yong Yeol, 63
AI. *See* Artificial intelligence
Antitrust regulation, 51, 80, 84
ARPANET, 125
Arrow, Kenneth, 95
Artificial intelligence (AI)
  in the 1960s, 13, 73–74
  in the 1980s, 13, 75–76
  in the 2000s, 13, 33, 78
  in the 2020s, 80–81
  auditing of, 33, 35, 36–37, 123–124, 126, 129, 132, 155–156n3
  augmenting bridging networks, 10, 42, 46, 49
  augmenting storytelling, 8, 14, 18, 28–30
  booms and busts, 71, 73
  and centralization, 68, 76–77, 85, 90, 112, 115, 119
  and communities, 33, 35, 83–84, 87
  in consensus networks, 12, 97, 119, 123–124, 132–133
  cooperative regulation of, 128–129
  and data ownership, 82–83, 84, 85
  and decision-making, 30–32, 33, 68, 87, 131
  and democracy, 16, 98–100
  ethical principles, 85–86, 98
  and ex-ante regulation, 130–131
  and governance, 16, 87–88, 99, 128
  governance for digital platforms, 126, 128
  and outcomes data, 126–127
  and prediction, 34, 65–66, 81, 85, 99
  and privacy, 10–11, 33, 35–36, 51, 82, 124
  role in society, 3–4, 13, 14, 17–18, 19, 121–122
  and storytelling, 18, 21, 25, 81–82, 86
  support systems and tools, 36–37, 87, 99
  unintended side effects, 15–16, 74, 76–77, 79–80, 82, 85, 119, 132
  use of stories, 5, 8, 72, 81
Auditing of AI behavior, 33, 35, 36–37, 123–124, 126, 129, 132, 155–156n3

Bakker, Michiel, 99
Bandit problem, 25
Bonding social capital, 14, 36, 48, 87
Braley, Alia, 46
Bridging networks, 8, 10, 18, 39–40, 41–42
  and child outcomes, 43, 46
  digital, 10–11
  and digital social networks, 49
  and innovation, 44–45, 58
  and poverty, 45–46
  and prosperity, 44–45
  and public policy, 41, 42

Bridging networks (cont.)
  and segregation, 46, 49
  and spread of new behaviors, 41
Bridging social capital, 14, 42, 48, 87
Bronze rule, 108

Caros, Nicholas, 44
Cascades
  physical, 137
  social, 137–138
Centralization
  and AI, 68, 76–77, 85, 90, 112, 115, 119
  in business, 51, 84
  and complexity, 78
  in governance, 59–60, 67–68, 107, 113–116, 124
  impact on innovation, 77–78
Chetty, Raj, 43
Child development, 42–43, 45, 46, 100
Citation networks, 63, 96, 97, 99–100
  and incentives, 12, 62–63
Citations, 11–12, 61, 62–65
Cities, 40–41, 44, 46, 90
  and bridging networks, 10, 39–41, 44, 46
  and innovation, 40–41
Citizen Stack, 118
Collaborative filtering, 78–79
Collective action
  and bridging networks, 10, 40, 45
  in community governance, 116–117
  and community intelligence, 6, 8, 23–24
  and consensus networks, 8, 11–12, 36, 124
  and democracy, 16, 46
  and digital platforms, 17, 19, 31, 52, 81–82, 91–93, 101, 121–122
  and dragons, 80, 91
  and shared wisdom, 6, 8–9, 87
  stories for change, 7, 35–36
  and trust, 115–116

Collective rationality, 28, 80, 85, 100
Commons
  definition of, 109
  governance of, 107–109, 112, 123
Community governance, 116–117
Community intelligence
  and abductive reasoning, 18
  in bees, 23, 24
  and bridging networks, 39–40
  compared to collective intelligence, 6
  and consensus networks, 12, 17, 53, 61–62, 64, 97, 104
  and cultural inventions, 8
  and digital support technologies, 15, 19, 32, 119
  and financial decision-making, 28, 30
  and minimum-regret decision-making, 25
  and story sharing, 5–7, 9, 17, 23–24, 87, 89, 119
Community search engines, 33
Consensus, 6, 8, 9, 11–12, 17–18, 23, 24, 63, 65, 112
Consensus networks
  and AI, 84, 86
  and community intelligence, 12, 17–18
  and deliberative platforms, 95–96
  and digital media, 66, 68, 95–96
  in governance, 87, 93, 107–109, 111, 114, 123–124
  in law, 63–65, 67, 99, 106–107
  Polis, 95–98, 99, 111
  and predicting innovation, 65–66
  in science, 11–12, 61–66, 111
  and story sharing, 11–12, 17–18, 53, 61, 121
  in technology development, 63–65, 67
  Uniform Law Commission, 36, 67, 106
Consensus organizations, 123–124, 126, 132–133
  key challenges, 126

INDEX

Consumer Reports, 51, 83, 118
Consumer Union, 51, 118. *See also* Consumer Reports
COVID, 41, 58, 92, 138
Cultural inventions, 3, 8, 11, 19
  augmented by AI, 8–9
  consensus networks, 11, 53, 66
  and the Enlightenment, 8, 12
  and innovation, 8, 19
  and story sharing, 3, 8, 11, 17–18, 19
Cybersecurity, 82, 125, 127

Data cooperatives, 51
Data ownership, 82–83, 84, 85, 117–118
Data trusts, 117–118, 130
Decision-making, 17–18, 19, 24–26, 31–32, 33, 87
  and digital support technologies, 31–32
  in finance, 27–30
  scaling of, 57–59, 68
  and story sharing, 57–58
Democracy
  and AI, 98–100
  and communities, 100–101
  and consensus networks, 61, 68
  definition of, 16, 89
  and deliberative platforms, 95–96, 98–99
  incentives for participation, 94
  and representatives, 56, 57
  and shared wisdom, 89
  and trust, 46–47
Digital deliberative platforms, 95–96, 98–99
Digital media
  as centralizing forces, 51, 68
  and data dragons, 49–51, 79–80
  role in society, 3–4, 15–16, 71, 88
  and shared wisdom, 9
  and social learning, 52–53
Digital social media, 72, 91, 123
Digital social networks, 49

Digital support technology, 31–36
  stories for change, 7, 12, 35–36, 93, 99
  stories for me, 34–35, 91–92, 99
  stories for ourselves, 7, 10, 32–34, 37, 51–52, 84, 92–93, 115
Disruption in social media, 91–92
Distributed digital systems, 112, 125
Dragons, 49–51, 52, 79–80, 118

Echo chambers, 9, 49, 52–53, 72, 79, 85, 119
Enhanced census data, 109–110
Enlightenment, the, vii, 8, 12, 55, 61, 90, 121, 131
Epstein, Ziv, 92
Ex-ante regulation, 123, 129–130
Expert systems, 75–76
Exploit-explore dilemma, 26, 48
Ex-post regulation, 123, 129

Financial decisions, 27–30, 37, 98
  in eToro, 27–29, 63
  by experts, 29–30
Four horsemen of social failure, 30, 60, 74–75, 138, 141–143
  gray swans, 75, 139, 141, 142
  myopia, 75, 140–141, 142
  one-size-fits-none, 75, 112, 114, 124, 139–140, 142
  unseen change, 75, 138–139, 142
Fragile Families Study, 42–43, 141
Friedman, John, 43

Governance, 16, 57, 59–60, 99, 101, 107–109, 113–114, 116, 128
Gray swans, 75, 139, 141, 142
  vs. black swans, 139

Hanseatic League, 56
Hero's journey, 4
Human agency, 19, 22, 30–32, 34, 36, 82, 95, 98–99
Hunter-gatherer bands, 9, 23, 25, 40

Incentives
  for consensus, 11–12, 62–63, 64–67, 94–95, 96–97, 106
  for participation, 93–94, 95
India Stack, 118
Innovation
  and bridging networks, 39, 42, 44–45, 58
  and centralization, 60–61, 77–78
  and cities, 40–41
  and consensus networks, 60–65
  and cultural inventions, 3, 8, 11
  prediction of, 65–66
  and social processes, 21
Intelligence, definition of, 5. *See also* Artificial intelligence; Community intelligence
International consensus organizations, 123–124, 126, 132–133
  challenges for, 126
Interoperability, 122, 128–129, 132

Kahneman, Daniel: system 1 and system 2 thinking, 24–25, 92–93
Kojaku, Sadamori, 63

Lera, Sandro, 63
Licklider, J. C. R., 14

Mahari, Robert, 63, 129
Marginalized communities, 93–94, 114
McChrystal, Stanley, 104
  team of teams, 104–106, 108, 114, 119
Mechanical model of society, 12, 59, 74, 90, 137, 138, 140, 141–142
Megill, Colin, 95. *See also* Polis
Minimum-regret decision-making, 25, 26, 28, 48, 63
Misinformation, 79, 81, 87, 92–93, 119
Moro, Esteban, 39, 45, 63
Myopia, 75, 140–141, 142

One-size-fits-none, 75, 112, 114, 124, 130, 139–140, 142
Opportunity Atlas, 43, 46
Ostrom, Elinor, 107–109. *See also* Commons
Ostrom's three principles, 108–113, 119, 126

Permission Slip, 51, 83, 118
Plato's "Noble Lie," 16, 56
Polis, 95–98, 99, 111
  in Taiwan, 96–97
Prediction markets, 95
Preferential attachment, 79, 80
Privacy, 10–11, 33, 35–36, 51, 52, 79, 82–83, 124, 127
  cryptography tools, 33, 35–36, 124, 127
  and data ownership, 51, 79, 82–83
Putnam, Robert, 115

Randomized controlled experiments (RCTs), 141
Rationality
  definition of, 28
  individual vs. collective, 28, 85, 100
RCTs, 141
Regulatory capture, 60
Representatives in government, 56–57, 58–59, 87, 100

Sampson, Robert, 46
SDGs, 110, 114, 126–127
Shared wisdom
  and bridging networks, 39
  and collective rationality, 28
  and consensus networks, 11, 17, 53
  and cultural inventions, 8, 11, 55
  definition of, 3, 5–6, 24
  and democracy, 89
  and digital media, 9, 32, 72
  improving, 17, 19
  and stories, 3, 5–6, 14, 17, 30

Smith, Adam, 13, 86
Social bridges, 39, 40, 46, 48–49, 52
Social influence, 87. *See also* Social learning
Social institutions
  reasons for failure, 12–13, 59–60
  redesigning of, 3, 14, 17–19, 36, 66, 68, 111–112, 115, 119, 131–132
Social learning, 8, 27–28, 48, 52–53, 87, 89–90
Social media
  digital, 72, 91, 123
  disruption in, 91–92
Songlines, 5, 22, 32
Stories
  and AI, 21, 25, 72, 81–82, 84, 86–87
  and community intelligence, 5–7, 9, 17, 23–24, 87, 89, 119, 142
  and consensus networks, 61, 63–65
  and decision-making, 31, 36, 56
  definition of, 6–7
  and intelligence, 5, 25
  role in learning, 21, 22–23, 27–28
  role in survival, 22, 23, 24
  and shared wisdom, 3, 5–6, 14, 17, 30
  and social bridges, 39, 40, 41
  story-sharing networks, 8, 9–12, 17–18, 19, 23–24, 28, 58, 84
  use of, 4–5
Stories for change, 7, 12, 35–36, 93, 99
Stories for me, 34–35, 91–92, 99
Stories for ourselves, 7, 10, 32–34, 37, 51–52, 84, 92–93, 115
Stories of the past, 4–5, 8, 22, 40, 55–56, 89–90, 103–105
Story-sharing networks, 9, 11, 17–18, 22–24, 27, 28–29, 30, 55, 142–143
Subversion dilemma, 46–47, 98
Symbiosis, 14
  vs. synergy, 14
Synergy between humans and technology, 14, 15, 21–22, 30–31, 36, 49–50, 121

Team of teams, 104–106, 108, 114, 119
Toyota quality circles, 105, 108
Trust, 46–47, 112, 114, 115–116, 117, 125, 127, 130
Tsai, Lily, 85–86, 91

UCC, 106, 108, 114
Uniform Law Commission, 36, 67, 106, 112, 119, 133
Unseen change, 75, 138–139, 142
UN Sustainable Development Goals (SDGs), 110, 114, 126–127
US Uniform Commercial Code (UCC), 106, 108, 114

Weak ties, effect of, 44, 87
Willer, Robb, 47
Wisdom, definition of, 5. *See also* Shared wisdom

Zheng, Jinhua, 42